RACE, RACISM AND THE DEATH PENALTY IN THE UNITED STATES

RACE, RACISM AND THE DEATH PENALTY IN THE UNITED STATES

Adalberto Aguirre, Jr.
and
David V. Baker

 VANDE VERE PUBLISHING LTD.

RACE, RACISM AND THE DEATH PENALTY
IN THE UNITED STATES

By

Adalberto Aguirre, Jr.

and

David V. Baker

Library of Congress Catalog Card Number

ISBN 0-9628916-5-7

DEDICATION

For my dad, Adalberto Aguirre,
he would have understood.

For my wife, Tina Marie,
she understands.

TABLE OF CONTENTS

FOREWORD

Race and ethnic relations in America are summarily portrayed as an essentially unchanging "internal colonial" pattern of white exploitation of minorities. Repressive discrimination in the criminal justice system is viewed as a key weapon used to enforce white dominance. In particular, it is argued that discriminatory use of the death penalty not only protects white interests but reinforces white racist attitudes. Lynchings and state executions are asserted to be historically complementary and functionally equivalent.

This small volume is packed with revealing evidence on how far short of "justice for all" our nation has fallen. There is no getting around the basic fact that racial biases, socioeconomic inequalities, and differential vulnerability to execution have been and continue to be linked. Whether our concerns begin with race and ethnic struggles, economic disparities, or the problems of crime and justice, we inevitably find that progress on one of these fronts depends upon progress on all of them. Our fraying social fabric cannot be mended one thread or piece at a time.

Let whoever disagrees with these authors' analyses and interpretations demonstrate wherein they are wrong. Even to provoke attention to the issues confronted here is itself an important contribution.

Austin T. Turk, Ph.D.
Professor and Chair
Department of Sociology
University of California, Riverside

ACKNOWLEDGEMENTS

We have accumulated a tremendous number of personal debts in the preparation of this book. In particular, during its writing we lost a friend and colleague, Professor Maurice Jackson, who kept reminding us that our work should be completed. It is not enough to say "Thank you" to Maurice because his advice and commentary resides throughout the pages of this book.

We appreciate the suggestions offered to us by Robert Hanneman and Charlie Case regarding the log-linear analysis. Our discussions with Alfredo Mirande, Ed Butler, Jon Turner, Richard Lowe, Deana Bustamonte, Ruben Martinez, and Jim Gier helped us iron out some of the wrinkles. In addition, the comments and suggestions offered by the anonymous reviewers were extremely useful in shaping our discussion. We also thank Leslie Villegas and Judy Lee for tracking down hard to find library source. Finally, we thank our families for their patience - Carmen, Tito, and Adrian -- Tina, Stacy, and Jeremy. We hope that this book will help our children understand a little bit more of the society they live in.

PREFACE

Writing this book has not been an easy task. As we discussed the ideas in this book with friends and colleagues we found out that the topic of "race" often produces extremely complex moral arguments. As we presented the ideas discussed in this book at scholarly meetings we also learned that "race-relation" is a topic oftentimes regarded as too burdensome for discussion. We hope this book will convince the reader that the discussion of "race" is a necessary requirement for understanding the sociological complexity of our society.

The principal objective of this book is not to portray United States society as a racist social system, but rather to examine the idea that the criminal justice system is rooted in racial inequality. On the one hand, we will show that the court system has applied the death penalty in a discriminatory manner to blacks. On the other hand, we will show that public support for the death penalty is characterized by prejudicial attitudes towards blacks. Thus, the criminal justice system facilitates the structural accommodation of blacks within a social ideology that perceives the death penalty as a vehicle for protecting white interests in society.

That day is a-comin' but we got to do certain things first. We need iron-clad lawmen, who ain't afraid to stand up for the principles this nation was founded on - One Nation Under God, yes-sir! - with white supremacy and justice for all! Now, as you probably know, I'm running for the office of sheriff. I'm not gonna abuse the privilege of my position as Exalted Cyclops to make a campaign speech, no, but I'll tell you this: there'll be no more arrests of white citizens who do their God-given duty when and if I'm elected. So if you want law and order and your rights as a white citizen protected, you'll vote for Farron Stroud. But if you want a lily-livered, niggerlovin', mammyjammin' sheriff you'll vote for my opponent. And that's about all I've got to say to you fellas tonight (Disch and Sladek, 1989:64).

b

The face in the criminal justice carnival mirror is also...very frequently a black face. Although blacks do not comprise the majority of the inmates in our jails and prisons, they make up a proportion that far outstrips their proportion in the population.... There can be little doubt that the criminal justice process is distorted by racism as well as by economic bias (Reiman, 1979:97).

ORGANIZATION OF THE BOOK

The book is divided into three parts: Part One investigates the extent to which the death penalty has been used as a mechanism to control blacks and thereby to keep blacks relegated to a subservient and subjugated social position to whites in order to protect white political, social, and economic interests. We begin in Chapter One with a review of the basic tenets of the internal colonial model of race and ethnic inequality. We attempt to incorporate these fundamentals into an explanation of why racial discrimination has characterized the imposition of the death penalty in the United States.

Many studies have documented evidence of racial discrimination in the imposition of the death penalty on blacks. In Chapter Two, the most important of these studies are reviewed in relation to whether they were conducted before, during the interim, or after the United States Supreme Court decisions in **Furman v. Georgia** (1972) and **Gregg v. Georgia** (1976). The pre-**Furman** studies basically show that the death penalty has been systematically applied in a discretionary manner against blacks. The studies conducted during the interim period (post-**Furman**, pre-**Gregg**) basically show that the **Furman** decision had little or no diminishing effect on the extent to which black capital offenders were subjected to racial discrimination in imposition of the death penalty. The post-**Gregg** studies further show that the death penalty remains disproportionately applied to blacks despite the Court's attempt to curb discriminatory use of the penalty. The findings reveal that extralegal (irrelevant) factors (social definitions) still enter into the judicial process to the extent that they influence the results of capital cases, and that the judicial guidelines designed to ensure that the death penalty is not applied in a capricious manner have failed to eliminate racial disparities in capital sentences.

Chapter Three specifically examines the historical development of racial discrimination in the imposition of the death penalty to blacks. A rich data source is analyzed in order to determine the degree of racial disparity in the application of the death penalty. The first source of data was compiled by Professor Negley K. Teeters with the assistance of Charles J. Zibulka, and was first published as an appendix to William J. Bowers' (1974) book entitled **Executions in America**. The Teeters-Zibulka data is an inventory of 5,708 executions conducted in the United States under state authority from 1853 to 1967. This data is comprised of the names of the persons executed, the dates of their executions, the states of execution, the counties of prosecution, the offense for which the prisoner was executed, the race and age of the person executed, and whether the prisoner was afforded an appeal of the case prior to execution. The importance of the Teeters-Zibulka data is not only that it lists "state-imposed" rather than local executions, but that it is not in aggregate form and, therefore, more sophisticated forms of data analysis can be employed to discern the specifics of interaction effects between the variables. The Teeters-Zibulka inventory is supplemented by the Richel-Munden inventory of 61 state-imposed executions in the United States from 1977 to 1986. These data contain the names of the prisoners executed, the state in which the execution took place, the method of execution, the race and age of the prisoner executed, and the date of execution.

Part Two focuses on the socio-cultural dimension of racial discrimination in the imposition of the death penalty to blacks. In this section, we measure the extent to which public support for the death penalty is characterized by prejudicial attitudes toward blacks. This analysis takes place on two dimensions of racial prejudice: the disproportionate lynching of blacks, and racial punitive attitudes toward blacks.

Chapter Four concerns the extent to which mob lynchings have characterized public sentiment toward blacks throughout a major portion of our nation's history. An attempt has been made to reconcile the several sources of data showing different numbers of blacks and whites lynched from 1882 to 1970. The chapter points out that along with the disproportionality factor, the inhuman bestiality associated with lynchings, the rationality of lynchings, and the degree of public support for the lynching of blacks have all worked to give notice to blacks that the white majority will not tolerate infringement upon its social, political, and economic interests. Evidence is presented which further shows that the lynching of blacks has not simply been relegated to the distant past, but that lynching is still an effective mechanism employed by whites to strike fear into the hearts of blacks who are perceived as threatening the interests of whites. Data on the number of persons lynched is also contrasted with the number of prisoners legally executed in the United States. This comparison tends to indicate that where mob violence left off, legal executions have taken over. That is, the locus of authority to execute social undesirables has simply transferred from the hands of the lynch mob to the power of the state.

Chapter Five amounts to a report on an empirical analysis that has been specifically designed to measure the extent to which public support for the death penalty is characterized by racial prejudice against blacks. This analysis examines the degree to which white racial prejudice against blacks affects people's attitudes toward the death penalty within a multivariate model including age, sex, level of educational attainment, geographical region, and whether the respondent fears criminal victimization. Racial prejudice is measured by a series of race relation questions. These variables reflect those demographics that are most often measured as determinants of public support for the death penalty. The study employs data from the National Opinion Research Center (NORC) 1984 General Social Survey (GSS). The method of data analysis entails the CATMOD (Log-linear Analysis of Categorical Data) procedure in SAS.

Finally, Part Three is a summary of our observations. In Chapter Six we review actions by the United States Supreme Court that have resulted in measures designed to sanction the discriminatory application of the death penalty to blacks. In Chapter Seven we attempt to synthesize our discussion in Chapters Two through Five regarding black/white race relations in the United States.

PART I

RACIAL DISCRIMINATION AND THE DEATH PENALTY: THE ROLE OF SOCIAL STRUCTURE

CHAPTER ONE

The Study of Racial and Social Inequality:
Some Preliminary Statements

Racial and social inequality are persistent features in American society. Despite the intention of those individuals that framed the Constitution to insure equal rights to every person, social differences have developed between persons during the historical maturation of the United States that have produced social, political, educational, and economic inequality (Pole, 1988). For example, according to Collier and Collier (1986) the framers of the Constitution faced a paradox in the distribution of equal rights on a state by state basis: will Negroes and Indians receive the same rights as the white man? As such, even the framers of the Constitution were fully aware of the differentiating effects race would have on the allocation of social and political rights to persons within states. As an ironic result, the Constitution is perceived by racial minorities as the vehicle for obtaining equal rights, and for limiting the scope of their rights (Fiss, 1986).

In an attempt to understand the dilemma social inequality poses for a society that espouses equal righs for all, sociologists have developed a set of conceptual approaches for the study of inequality - in particular, racial and ethnic inequality (Yinger, 1985). The presence of racial and ethnic inequality in a society that commits itself to individual rights is a direct challenge to the historical romanticism surrounding the adaptation of immigrants to United States society. For example, it is assumed that recognition of an individual's rights in American society transcends his or her racial and ethnic group membership. Regarding this issue, Takaki (1979) has noted that race and ethnicity have played a significant historical role in determining the individual rights of certain racial and ethnic immigrant groups in United States society. Thus, to borrow an observation from C. Wright Mills in **The Sociological Imagination** (1959), the study of race and ethnic inequality in the United States becomes the sociologist's quest for an introspective understanding of equality in American society.

CONCEPTUAL APPROACHES TO THE STUDY OF INEQUALITY

Barrera (1979) has identified the following general categories for conceptual approaches that focus on racial and ethnic inequality: **deficiency theories** - racial and ethnic minorities are viewed as occupying inferior economic, social, and political positions in United States society due to biological, cultural or social deficiencies in the minority group; **bias theories** - prejudice and discrimination by white persons are viewed as the primary sources of inequality for minority persons; **structural discrimination theories** - racial and ethnic inequality is located in the distribution of social rewards and opportunities within the social structure of United States society as a whole. In contrast, Feagin (1984) classifies approaches to the study of racial and ethnic inequality into either one of two categories: **order theories** - racial and ethnic inequality is viewed as a necessary condition for the maintenance and protection of power and privilege in United States white society; **power-conflict theories** - racial and ethnic inequality is viewed as necessary for the creation of privilege in white United States society. (See Feagin and Feagin, 1978:1-18.) Regardless of how one classifies an approach to the study of racial and ethnic inequality, the attempt is to link individual social features to social structures of power, privilege, and control that determine unequal social relations in society.

THE INTERNAL COLONIAL APPROACH

The conceptual approach to the study of social inequality that guides our discussion in the following chapters of this book is the **Internal Colonial Model** of racial and ethnic inequality.

Casanova (1965:33) defines internal colonialism as: "(c)orresponding to a structure of social relations based on domination and exploitation among culturally heterogeneous, distinct groups." According to Marguia (1975) and Jinadu (1976) the internal colonial model makes possible the study of the historical development of unequal social relations based on race and ethnicity, and the study of political and economic colonialization based on race and ethnicity.[1] One of the most systematic and rigorous applications of the internal colonial model to racial and ethnic inequality in the United States is Mario Barrera's (1979) examination of the historical development of race and class in the Mexican American population of the American Southwest.[2] The model developed by Barrera (1979:196) to study the colonial situation of Mexican Americans in the American Southwest is outlined in Figure 1.

According to Figure 1, the most salient features in the internal colonial model that promote and transmit racial and ethnic inequality are **interests** and **racial prejudice**. According to Barrera (1979:196): "The interests here are those which originally gave rise to European colonialism, of which internal colonialism is an extension, as well as the contemporary interests of privileged groups." These interests can be traced back to historical periods when European powers sought new trade markets and raw materials. For example, from the early seventeenth to the mid-nineteenth century the United States expanded its mercantilist interests (e.g. search for raw materials) by developing trade routes that provided a developing Southern plantation economy with a cheap form of labor - namely, African slaves. As a cheap form of labor, then, slavery became important for the white plantation owners because it provided them with a means for generating profit. In turn, the system of social relations that emerged between slave and plantation owner established a system of structural discrimination that promoted the privileged status of the plantation owner. In addition, the privileged status of the plantation owner was shielded by the use of sanctions (i.e. lynchings) to control persons, namely slaves, that would threaten the interests of the plantation owner.

In a related example, Chambliss (1964) has studied the emergence of vagrancy statutes to demonstrate that vagrancy laws were designed to guarantee the established elites (landowners) with a sufficient force of cheap labor during the Black Death. In the same study, Chambliss also demonstrates how vagrancy laws were employed as secondary mechanisms for protecting the property of landowners. In summary, the interests of the privileged members in society - landowners, plantation owners, etc. - are protected by vesting social structure with the interests of the privileged in the maintenance of structural discrimination vis-a-vis the use of sanctions (i.e. lynchings, laws, head taxes, etc.).

Figure 1

The Internal Colonial Model (Blauner, 1972; Barrera, 1979)

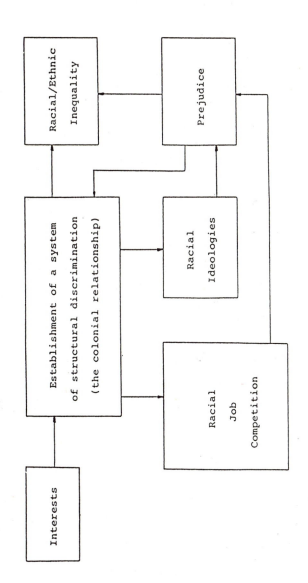

The second important feature in Figure 1 is **racial prejudice** as the product of racial ideologies. As noted in Figure 1, a system of structural discrimination leads to racial ideologies that, in turn, lead to racial prejudice. According to Barrera (1979), unlike the colonial relationship between the interests of the privileged group in society and the development of a system of structural discrimination, racial ideologies cannot be traced back to ancient times, and are, as a result, a modern phenomenon. This is not to argue, however, that ethnocentrism (e.g. the belief that one's own ethnic group is superior to others) does not have historical roots beyond the modern era. Barrera explains that ethnocentric beliefs have been traditionally justified on cultural grounds and not on the idea that other groups are inherently and biologically (genetically) inferior. However, racial ideologies did not develop until the nineteenth century when European aristocrats were attempting to secure their own social position (Barrera, 1979:198):

> "...[T]hese ideologies took the position that the aristocrats were descendants of the Germanic peoples (referred to as Teutons and later as Aryans) (Caucasians) who had overrun the old Roman Empire. The common people, on the other hand, were depicted as descendants of other, inferior European stocks, including the Romans. The aristocrats were thus the descendants of a race which had provided its superiority in the distant past, and which had subsequently been responsible for the advance of civilization. By virtue of this inheritance they were ideally suited to rule and to maintain their class privileges. Later on, racist ideologies were transformed in Europe in order to serve the interests of nationalism, as France and Germany struggled for supremacy on the continent.... In England, the origins of racist ideologies can be traced back to the sixteenth century and the creation of the Church of England. As the English delved more deeply into their past, they began to idealize their past political as well as religious institutions, and to link them historically to the institutions that had existed among the Teutonic people to whom they traced their ancestry. In the early stages this school of thought was not explicitly racial, but seemed to assume that the superiority of the old institutions had simply been transmitted over the generations."

In the United States, racial ideologies became the basis for justifying the exploitative relationships between black slaves and white southern plantation owners. Gunnar Myrdal (1972:88), however, notes that "...when the Negro was first enslaved, this subjugation was not justified in terms of his biological inferiority." Rather, the racial ideology developed as a pro-slavery response to moral questioning of the "universal rights of man." (See Barrera, 1979:200.) The doctrine of biological inequality between blacks and whites became a convenient solution to the problem "...where the South wanted to defend a political and civic institution of inequality which showed increasingly greater prospects for new land exploitation and commercial profit, but where they also wanted to retain the democratic creed of the nation..." (Myrdal, 1944:87-88). That is, the biological inequality thesis enabled the southern plantation owners a means of justifying institutionalized slavery in the face of democratic principles. This was not so difficult a task in light of the idea that although the Constitution did not specifically mention slavery, the Constitution did legitimize slavery. For example, Litward (1987) has noted that the racial values and attitudes of the Founding Fathers were those of most Americans, among them the assumption that blacks were culturally and genetically unsuited for democracy. In addition, Litward notes that the **Dred Scot** decision attests to the historical truths of such beliefs. He notes that the Supreme Court declared in that decision that the Constitution's authors felt blacks "...had no rights which the white man was bound to respect."

Once the Civil War had been fought and the agitations between northern industrialists and southern plantation owners had subsided, the racial ideology "...intensified as a means of justifying the continued exploitation of the black population" (Barrera, 1979:201). But the racial ideology was not limited to the South. Myrdal (1944:88) points out that "...the ideology became more prevalent in the North as a way of justifying the national compromise arrived at in the 1870's that allowed the South to continue its oppression of the Blacks."

Racism and its racist ideologies remain pervasive in contemporary American society because they are deeply ingrained in its culture. Barrera (1979:201) explains that "...(r)acial ideologies become embodied in the thought of future generations who have no conception of the exact context in which they originated, and are thus transformed into broad-based racial prejudice even among people whose interests are not served by it." Cox (1970:333) adds to this viewpoint in arguing that race prejudice has become part of our cultural heritage and that "...as such both exploiter and exploited for the most part are born heirs to it." These observations reinforce the idea that racial prejudice and the ideology of racism in contemporary American society are "irrational, ingrained racial folklore at work." As Litwack (1987) has noted, "racism in American society remains pervasive because new civil rights laws...failed to diminish the violence of poverty...to reallocate resources, to redistribute wealth and income...[and] to penetrate the corporate boardrooms and federal bureaucracies...."

A CONCEPTUAL LINK: Internal Colonialism and Racial Prejudice

One can observe in Figure 1 that Barrera has introduced the notion of "racial job competition" as a necessary link for the maintenance of racial prejudice. According to Barrera (19779:196-198), the notion of "racial job competition" is operationalized when employers attempt to undercut the wages of white workers by creating a colonized labor pool. The colonized labor pool consists of persons that already find themselves in colonized social environments (i.e., ghettos, barrios, etc.) within United States society - namely, ethnic and racial minorities. However, instead of retaliating against employees for hiring workers from a colonized labor pool, white workers focus their frustration on racial and ethnic group members. As a result, racial and ethnic persons are perceived as a visible threat by white workers. In turn, white workers internalize their perceptions regarding racial and ethinic persons into a general belief system that supports racial prejudice against racial and ethnic persons.

Since our purpose in this book is to utilize the explanatory power of the internal colonial model regarding our analysis of the relationship between race and the death penalty in the United States criminal justice system, we have adjusted Barrera's model as outlined in Figure 2. First, in Figure 2 one can observe that the legal and illegal execution (lynching) of black persons is: (a) the result of socio-structural arrangements in United States society that place black persons at a greater social risk regarding executions; and (b) necessary to the maintenance of racial ideologies and racial prejudice that constrain black persons to limited socio-structural arrangements in United States society. Regarding our purpose in this book then, it is imperative that we examine the relationship between racial prejudice toward black persons and support for the death penalty. If a relaitonship is present between these two dimensions then one may assume that racial prejudice plays an important role in determining general attitudes toward the use of capital punishment with racial and ethnic persons. We present this analysis in chapter six.

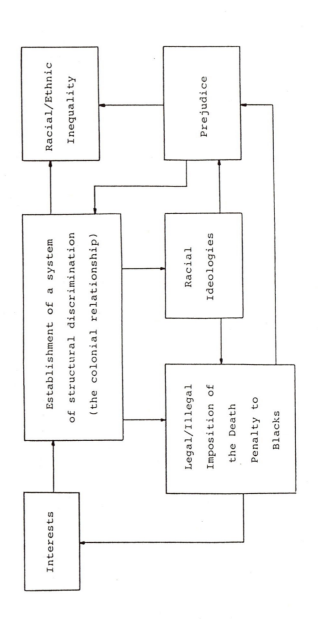

Figure 2

The Internal Colonial Model (Revised)

Secondly, we have linked the legal and illegal executions of black persons directly to "interests" because it is our argument in this book that the death penalty has been disproportionately applied to black persons in United States society. Given the interactive role the legal and illegal execution of black persons plays in maintaining discriminatory and prejudiced racial ideologies toward black persons, one would then expect for the legal and illegal execution of black persons to be a symbolic justification for maintaining dominant group interests in United States society. That is, we are not suggesting that United States society - in particular, white society - is by definition racially prejudiced against black persons. Rather, we are suggesting that racial ideologies have developed to support the interests of white society from ethnic and racial persons, and that capital punishment (e.g., the death penalty) is a vehicle for protecting the interests of white society from black persons. If our observations are valid, then we would expect to find that the death penalty has been disproportionately applied to black persons when compared to white persons. We present this analysis in chapter three.

Finally, we want to stress to the reader that our purpose in this book is not to test the application of the internal colonial model in our analysis of the relationship between race and the death penalty in the United States. We have selected the internal colonial model as an explanatory tool in our attempt to examine the socio-cultural nature of capital punishment and racial ideology in United States society. As an explanatory tool, the internal colonial model is important to our purposes in this book because: "A well-developed theory formulates what constitutes a fixed set of conditions, and thus provides direction for assessing observations...a theory provides guidance by defining the appropriate research situation for answering the questions posed by the theory's derivations" (Cohen, 1980:187). Thus, we believe that the internal colonial model is an important conceptual approach to an examination of how the socio-cultural structure of a society provides for and implements social mechanisms that seek to control social members - namely, to colonize black persons vis-a-vis the death penalty.

CHAPTER TWO

RACIAL DISCRIMINATION AND THE IMPOSITION
OF THE DEATH PENALTY TO BLACKS

The United States Bureau of Justice Statistics (1985) reports that between 1930 and 1984 there were 3,891 prisoners executed under civil authority in the United States. Of these figures, 2,067 (53.1%) were black, 1,773 (45.5%) were white and 42 (1.0%) of other races. Theere were 1,640 (48.7%) black persons, and 1,686 (50.8%) white persons executed for murder. Racial disparity in imposing the death penalty becomes even more clearly defined among executions for rape. Of the 455 executions for rape during this period, 89% (405) were of blacks and 10.5% (48) were of whites. The South executed 98.3% (398) of all blacks executed for rape. While the north central region of the country executed the remaining seven blacks executed for rape, the western and northwestern sections have never executed a black prisoner for rape. The District of Columbia, Virginia, West Virginia, Mississippi, Louisiana, and Oklahoma have never executed a white for the crime of rape.

Given that blacks have consistently represented about 11% of the total United States population since 1930, these statistics overwhelmingly indicate that the death penalty has been dispropor-tionately applied to blacks. Blacks executed for murder constitute over five times the rate of executions for whites, and blacks have been executed for rape about nine times the rate of execution than whites. These statistics alone do not show that racial discrimination has characterized the imposition the death penalty to blacks. But a number of empirical studies have shown that in the case of blacks, disproportionality in the application of the death penalty amounts to racial discrimination. The purpose in this chapter, then, is to review the empirical studies that have established rather pervasive evidence that the death penalty has not only been disproportionately applied to blacks convicted of rape and murder, but that the death penalty has been imposed on black prisoners in a discretionary and discriminatory manner. This review will clearly illustrate that racial discrimination has become so well entrenched and routinized in imposing the penalty of death on blacks that it has developed into a "systematic pattern of differential treatment" of blacks.

Many studies have documented evidence of racial discrimination in the imposition of the death penalty on blacks. These studies will be reviewed in terms of whether they were conducted before, during the interim, or after the United States Supreme Court decisions in **Furman v. Georgia** (1972) and **Gregg v. Georgia** (1976). The **Furman** decision basically held that all death penalty statutes in the United States were unconstitutional because they permitted the death penalty to be applied in a discretionary and discriminatory manner and amounted to "cruel and unusual punishment" in violation of the Eighth Amendment to the U.S. federal Constitution. The **Furman** decision did not abolish capital punishment in the United States; the court argued that the death penalty "in and of itself" does not constitute cruel and unusual punishment, but, the capricious manner in which the penalty had been applied in the cases before the Court at the time of **Furman** was held unconstitutional. In the **Gregg** decision, the Court attempted to curb the extent to which the death penalty was applied to blacks in a discretionary and discriminatory manner by providing for guided discretion in capital sentencing. The Court affirmed the death sentences of the cases under review in **Gregg** because the states from which the cases originated, in their capital statutes, had directed attention on the circumstances of the crimes and provided for consideration of mitigating factors designed to protect against arbitrary imposition of the death penalty.

PRE-FURMAN STUDIES

The earliest study conducted on black-white differentials in the administration of justice was completed by Brearley in 1930. Brearley found that of the 407 homicides in South Carolina between 1920 and 1926, 52% of the accusations resulted in guilty verdicts. Of these convictions, 64% involved blacks and 32% involved whites. Brearley (1930:252) attributes this finding to "such factors as race prejudice by white jurors and court officials and the Negro's low economic status, which prevents him from securing 'good' criminal lawyers for his defense." (See also Sellin, 1980:56-57).

As early as 1933, Myrdal reported that in ten southern states: "The Negro constitutes less than thirty percent of the population in these states, but has more than twice as many death sentences imposed. Actual executions make the racial differential still greater, for 60.9% of the Negro death sentences were carried out as compared with 48.7% of the white." (Quoted in Bowers, 1974:109).

In 1940, Mangum studied racial disparities in imposing the death penalty in several southern states. In his book **The Legal Status of the Negro**, Mangum reports that for the years 1920 to 1938, 74% of the blacks and 50% of the whites sentenced to death were executed. In 1938, Missouri executed 83% of the blacks and 75% of the whites who were sentenced to death. From 1909 to 1938, Mangum reports that 52% of the blacks and 39% of the whites sentenced to death were executed. In Oklahoma from 1915 to 1937, 39% of the blacks and 34% of the whites were executed, while South Carolina executed 72% of the blacks and 41% of the whites who had been sentenced to death from 1912 to 1938. Mangum further found that between 1928 and 1938, Tennessee executed 67% of the blacks and 35% of the whites sentenced to death, and Virginia executed 61% of the blacks and 42% of the whites sentenced to death. Texas was found to have executed 83% of the blacks and 79% of the whites who had been sentenced to death from 1924 to 1938.

Another early study on race and capital punishment was conducted by Johnson in 1941. For the period 1930 to 1940, Johnson studied 220 homicide cases in Richmond, Virginia, 95 homicide cases in Fulton County, Georgia, and 330 homicide cases from five counties in North Carolina. Johnson basically found that the "Negro versus Negro offenses are treated with undue leniency, while the Negro versus white offenses are treated with undue severity" (1941:98). The death penalty was most often imposed on blacks whose victims were white, and least likely applied to blacks whose victims were black. For example, in Virginia and Georgia, Johnson reports that 27% of the black offenders whose victims were white received the death penalty, while only 16% of the white offenders with white victims, and 3% of the black offenders with black victims received the death penalty. Further, no white offender whose victim was black received the death penalty.

Allredge (1942) reported that conviction rates for criminal himicide dramatically differed for blacks and whites in seven regions of the South from 1940 to 1941. Allredge found that 89% of the blacks accused of murdering whites were convicted; 67% of the blacks accused of killing blacks were convicted; 64% of the whites accused of murdering whites were convictèd; and only 43% of the whites accused of murdering blacks were convicted.

In 1949, Garfinkel also established that there was a statistically significant association between the race of the defendant and the race of the victim. Garfinkel investigated 821 homicide cases in ten counties in North Carolina between 1930 and 1940. He found that the race of the defendant and that of the victim were demonstrable factors in imposing the death penalty: 94% of the blacks who killed whites were indicted for first degree murder, compared to 28% of the whites accused of killing blacks. Only 15% of the blacks accused of killing whites were acquitted. Garfinkel found that while 10% of the blacks who killed whites received life imprisonment, none of the whites who killed blacks received life imprisonment.

Johnson (1957) studied rape cases resulting in the application of the death penalty in North Carolina between 1909 and 1954. He found that 56% of all persons executed during this period were black, and 43% were white. Johnson's study basically concluded that blacks were far more likely to suffer the death penalty for rape than were whites convicted of rape.

The Florida Civil Liberties Union reported similar findings from a study conducted in that state in 1964. In Florida between 1940 and 1964, 54% (45) of the black males who raped white women, but none of the eight white males convicted of raping a black female, received th4e death penalty.

A study conducted by the Ohio Legislative Service Commission in 1961 found that 37% of all Ohio death penalty sentences during 1950 were rendered upon black offenders, and that whites more often had their sentences commuted to life imprisonment when compared to blacks.

Wolfgang et al.'s (1962) study of 439 men sentenced to death in Pennsylvania for murder between 1914 and 1958 found it statistically significant that only 11% of the convicted blacks had their sentences commuted to life imprisonment, while 20% of the white prisoners had their sentences commuted. (See also Wolfgang and Riedel, 1973.)

A variety of other researchers have found that the death penalty has been disproportionately applied to blacks in several other states. Center and Smith (1969) found that executions of blacks comprised 22% (41) of all executions in California for the 25-year period between 1938 and 1963. It should be noted that 82.9% of those blacks executed in California were born in southern states. (See also Judson et al., 1969; and compare Kalven, 1969.) Similarly, Koeninger (1969) found that in Texas it is the black, the young, the poor, and the ignorant who have been disproportionately executed. Koeninger found that of the 460 persons executed in Texas between 1924 and 1968 58.5% were black. Of the 341 persons executed for murder, 52.8% were black, and of the 108 executions for rape, 77.8% were black. Koeninger (1969:141) also points out that in many instances where a white and black were co-defendants, "the white was sentenced to life imprisonment or a term of years, and the Negro was given the death penalty." (See also Ehrmann, 1952; McCafferty, 1972.)

In March of 1972, Wolfgang testified before Subcommittee No. 3 of the Committee on the Judiciary of the United States House of Representatives on legislation proposed for a moratorium on capital punishment (Hart-Cellar Hearings, March 16, 1972:174-180, 182, 183). Wolfgang's testimony was later published in William J. Bowers' Executions in America (1974). (See also Wolfgang and Reidel, 1975; Coker v. Georgia, 1977.) The testimony presented evidence supporting the contention of racial discrimination in the imposition of the death penalty. With the aid of the NAACP Legal Defense and Education Fund, Inc., and Professor Anthony Amsterdam, Wolfgang collected data on over 3,000 cases of convictions of rape between 1945 and 1965 in 250 counties in 11 southern states: Alabama, Arkansas, Florida, Georgia, Louisiana, Mississippi, North Carolina, South Carolina, Tennessee, Texas, and Virginia.

Beyond examining "whether race was associated with the imposition of the death penalty for blacks convicted of rape," Wolfgang and his associates "were interested in determining whether non-racial factors could account for the higher proportions of blacks sentenced to death." Over two dozen variables were designed to measure non-racial factors concerning disproportionate application of the death penalty of blacks.   These variables included issues about the circumstances of the offense (the degree of force employed by the defendant to effectuate the crime, the amount of physical harm suffered by the victim, and whether the crime was committed in the course of committing another crime); the character of the victim (age, marital status, dependent children, chastity); characteristics of the defendant (age, marital status, occupation, prior criminal record); the nature of the relationship between the defendant and the victim (prior acquaintance, prior sexual relations); and the circumstances surrounding the trial that lead to the conviction of the defendant.

Wolfgang's findings were startling. Not one of the several non-racial variables "could account for the higher proportion of blacks sentenced to death upon conviction of rape." (That is, none of the several variables were found to be statistically significant at the .05 level of confidence using the chi-square test of statistical significance.) This finding held true whether the analysis was performed on individual states or for composite analysis combining several states. Race was the only variable found to be statistically significant. Wolfgang's conclusion from this finding was that only race could account for the disproportionate application of the death penalty to blacks convicted of rape.

Zimring et al. (1976) collected data on 204 homicide cases in Philadelphia in 1970. Among all felony killings reported to police during that year, 65% of the black defendants convicted of killing a white were sentenced to death or life imprisonment. But of those felony defendants convicted of killing blacks, only 25% were sentenceed to death or life imprisonment. These findings must be understood in light of the fact that fewer than 20% of the cases analyzed were homicides that had interracial combinations of defendant/victim. Zimring et al. conclude from these findings that "[t]hose who are least likely to be killed are most protected by sentencing policy" (1976:233).

Kleck (1981), who has critically evaluated the studies on racial discrimination in the use of the death penalty conducted prior to the **Furman** decision makes two observations about these various studies. First, he argues that while there are conclusive patterns of racial discrimination against blacks in the imposition of the death penalty, these patterns are mostly restricted to the imposition of the death penalty in southern states. On this point, however, Kleck is incorrect. While racial disparities in imposing the penalty of death are more pronounced in the South, studies by the Ohio Legislative Service Commission (1961), Wolfgang, et al. (1962), Zimring, et al. (1976), Carter and Smith (1969), Kalven (1969), Bowers and Pierce (1980), Bedau (1964, 1965), and Gross & Mauro (1984, 1989) have shown that patterns of racial discrimination in presentencing, sentencing, and postsentencing decisions on who suffers imposition of harsher punishments are not simply relegated to the southern jurisdictions. (See also Hagan and Burmiller, 1983). Gross and Mauro (1984), in fact, have commented on Kleck's conclusion. They note that "[t]o say there is no racial discrimination in capital sentencing, except in the South, is a bit like saying that there is no housing discrimination in a metropolitan area, except in the major residential district," (Gross and Mauro, 1984:42, note 61).

The second observation made by Kleck is that black defendants who murder black victims are the least likely defendant-victim category associated with the death penalty outside of the South. This observation has substantial merit, as noted above. In attempting to explain the apparently lenient treatment of black defendants convicted of murdering a black victim, Kleck suggests that "interracial crimes...are considered by [the] predominantly white social-control agents to be less serious offenses, representing less loss or threat to the community than crimes with white victims" (1981:800).

Review of pre-**Furman** studies on capital punishment demonstrates that the death penalty was systematically applied to black defendants in a discretionary and discriminatory manner. We have seen that this practice has not simply been relegated to the South, but that racial discrimination in the use of the death penalty has been a national characteristic. Moreover, these various studies illustrate the extent to which racism has permeated the criminal justice institution in the United States. Bowers and Pierce (1980) argue that this pattern of racial discrimination in imposing the death penalty to blacks has been an integral part of the American criminal justice system since before the Civil War. They note several states had passed legislative ordinances during the early part of the nineteenth century specifically requiring the death penalty to be used on blacks for particular crimes for which whites received only a prison sentence. The Virginia Assembly, for example, passed a statue in 1848 that provided for the death penalty to be used on blacks for any offense that was punishable by three or more years imprisonment for whites. (Bowers, 1974; **Virginia Law Review**, 1972; **Jackson v. Georgia**, 1972).

THE INTERIM PERIOD (post-Furman, pre-Gregg)

Several studies have been conducted on racial discrimination during the interim period after **Furman** was decided by the United States Supreme Court in 1972, but before the Court handed down its decision in **Gregg** in 1976. One of the most important studies conducted during this period compared the racial composition of prison death row inmates under the sentence of death in December 1971 (pursuant to pre-**Furman** capital statues) with offenders under sentence of death as of December 1975 (pursuant to mandatory and discretionary post-**Furman** capital stutes). Reidel (1976) not only found that the racial disparities of death row inmates in the pre-**Furman** era remained unchanged in the post-**Furman** period, but also that black defendants-white victims was the racial category with the highest rate of death sentences imposed. Reidel reported that 53% of the death row inmates in December 1971 were nonwhite, and that this figure rose to 62% in December 1975. While the racial disparity of death rows in the South had declined from 67% to 63% during this period, the western region of the United States increased its degree of racial disparity of black/white death row inmates from 26% to 52%. From these figures, Reidel concluded that statutes enacted before or after the **Furman** decision produced the same degree of racial disproportion in death sentences.

Reidel also found that 87% of the death sentences were for white-victim murders, and 45% were for the murder of white victims by black defendants. The degree of racial disparity in death sentences is even more pronounced in this period (1971-1975), and the white victim-black defendant category comprised the smallest proportion of the total number of murder cases.

In a study of first degree murder prosecutions in Dade County, Florida, from 1973 to 1976, Arkin (1980) reported that black defendants who murdered whites were more likely to be sentenced to death than white defendants. Arkin's data reveal that black offenders who killed whites were convicted of first-degree murder about four times more often than blacks who killed blacks. While the black offender/white victim category of criminal offense comprised only 21% of the 350 murder cases prosecuted, 50% of the cases resulting in death penalty sentences came from that category of offender. (See also Boris, 1969; Swigert and Farrell, 1976, 1977; Gross and Mauro, 1984:43, note 69; Bowers, 1983; Gross (1985.)

In sum, these studies show that the **Furman** decision had little or no effect on diminishing the extent to which black capital offenders were subjected to racial discrimination in imposing the death penalty. As noted, the **Furman** decision ruled that discrimination in applying the death penalty is blatantly unconstitutional. These studies, however, show that the death penalty was still used as a mechanism by which to particularly protect a specific class of individual - namely, whites - from criminal victimization.   Black defendants whose victims were white were overwhelmingly convicted and sentenced to death when compared to other racial categories of defendant-victim.   **Furman** had no demonstrable effect on the manner in which the death penalty was being applied in this country.

POST-GREGG STUDIES

In **Gregg**, the United States Supreme Court upheld the constitutionality of the death penalty for murder. The Court affirmed the convictions because the states from which the capital cases originated had provided for: bifurcated trials (one trial to establish guilt of the defendant, and another trial to determine an appropriate sentence); consideration of mitigating circumstances of the defendant and the crime; and appellate review of the capital sentences. These guidelines were affirmed by the court because they were specifically designed to prevent arbitrary and discriminatory imposition of the death penalty. It should be noted that in **Woodman v. North Carolina** (1976) and **Roberts v. Louisiana** (1976), decided the same day as **Gregg**, the court declared that the capital punishment statues in North Carolina and Louisiana were blatantly unconstitutional because they "allowed no room for consideration of individual mitigating circumstances and "the jury's power to determine the degree of the crime in light of the mandatory penalty for first-degree murder did not safeguard against the arbitrary and capricious imposition of the death sentences" (**Woodman v. North Carolina**, 1976:280).

Within the past few years, empirical analyses have revealed that the guidelines established in **Gregg** have failed to eliiminate racial disparities in capital cases. One of the most extensive studies performed on data collected after the **Gregg** decision was conducted by Bowers and Pierce (1980). Bowers and Pierce examined patterns of death sentencing in Florida, Texas, Ohio, and Georgia from 1972 to 1977. (It is interesting to note that 70% of all death sentences imposed in the United States from 1972 to 1977 were issued by these states). Basically, Bowers and Pierce found that the decision to execute in these states reflects the arbitrariness and discrimination that has characterized the imposition of the death penalty in the past (before the **Furman** and **Gregg** decisions). In each of these states, Bowers and Pierce found that killers of whites were more likely to be sentenced to death than killers of blacks, and that black defendants with white victims were more likely to receive the death penalty than white defendants with black victims. In Florida, black defendants with white victiims were found to have a 22% chance of being sentenced to death; white defendants with white victims had a 20% chance; and black defendants with black victims had a 0.6% chance of suffering imposition of the death penalty. It should be noted that in Florida, no white was sentenced to death for the killing of a black. Georgia and Texas were found to have somewhat lower rates of death sentences according to defendant-victim categories, but the pattern of racial discrimination in imposing the death penalty in particular defendant-victim racial combinations still prevailed. (See also Ekland-Olson, 1988.) More specifically, black defendants with white victims were eight times more likely to be sentenced to death than black defendants with black victims. In addition, Florida prosecutors overcharged non-felony homicide cases involving black killers of white victims as felony homicides. Bowers and Pierce have pointed out that the data on felony homicides suggests that "in black offender-white victim cases prosecutors may have alleged felony circumstances to enhance their plea bargaining positions or as a demostration of concern for the kinds of crimes the community finds most shocking" (1980:612). Likewise, in Florida and Georgia, appellate review of capital sentences did not correct for patterns of racial discrimination in imposing death to blacks. Thus, the guidelines established in **Gregg** have "become the instruments of arbitrariness and discrimination, not their cure" (Bowers and Pierce, 1980:629).

Radelelt (1981) examined whether race remained a significant factor in the processing and outcome of post-**Furman** homicide cases in 20 Florida counties in 1976 and 1977. He discovered that blacks accused of murdering whites were more likely to be sentenced to death than blacks accused of murdering blacks. This trend is explained by Radelet as due primarily to higher probabilities of blacks accused of murdering whites to be indicted for first-degree murder. When controlling for the race of the victim, however, Radelet's data did not clearly support the hypothesis that the race of the defendant is strongly associated with the probability of a first-degree murder indictment or imposition of the death penalty. Rather, "relative equality in the imposition of the death penalty appears mythical as long as prosecutors are more likely to obtain first-degree murder indictments for those accused of murdering white strangers than for those accused of murdering black strangers" (1981:926). Thus, Radelet's study tends to indicate that racial discrimination is alive and well in Florida's criminal justice system to the extent that a lower value is placed on the lives of black persons than on the lives of white persons.

In 1981, Zeisel published his analysis of the Sheppard-Carithers data on the composition of Florida death rows from 1972 to 1981. Zeisel found Florida continues to discriminate against black defendants convicted of killing which victims in imposing the death penalty. Zeisel points out that this pattern of systematic discrimination based on the race of the defendant and the victim is consistent with pre-**Furman** studies: the percentage of offenders on Florida's death rows who killed blacks (12%) was still considerably below the 47% who had killed whites. To Zeisel, prosecutors have considerable discretionary powers in determining the death row population and that this discretionary power does not appear to be "within any legal boundaries" (1981:468).

Using data on 1400 homicide cases in some 32 Florida counties between 1973 and 1977, Radelet and Pierce (1983) examined disparities between police reports and court records on "felony," "possible felony," and "non-felony" homicides. Among racial combinations of defendant-victim, black defendants who killed white victims were considerably more likely to have their cases upgraded to a felony charge and least likely to have their cases downgraded to a lesser charge as they moved through the judicial process. (See also Gross and Mauro, 1984).

In South Carolina, Paternoster (1983) found that when the race of the offender and the race of the victim are considered together, a clear pattern of racial disparity in prosecutors' decisions to seek the death penalty is evidenced. Paternoster argued that substantial racial disparity continues to exist in that blacks who kill whites have over a 4.5 times greater risk of having the death penalty sought than do black killers of blacks. Whites who kill blacks are only slightly (1.12 times) more likely to have the death penalty sought by the prosecutor than whites who kill other whites. The race of the victim appears to be a more important consideration of public prosecutors than is the race of the offender, concludes Paternoster. Hence, post-**Furman** capital punishment statutes fail to remedy the problem of racial discrimination influencing imposition of the death penalty in capital cases. (See also Jacoby and Paternoster, 1982; Paternoster, 1984.)

Radelet and Vandiver (1983) examined the degree to which the Florida Supreme Court has achieved the goals of "consistency and fairness" in capital sentencing. They were also concerned with whether the extralegal factors of the defendant's race and/or the victim's sex correlate with the court's decision to uphold the death sentence of a convicted capital offender. Their concern arose from Justice Brennan and Marshall's dissenting opinion in **Proffit** (1976) that a state supreme court's review of capital sentences would ensure "even-handed and consistent" application of the death penalty sentences. Radelet and Vandiver found, however, that out of the 145 death sentence cases examined by the Florida Supreme Court, 51.7% (76) were affirmed. Of the 70 remaining cases resulting in a favorable decision for the defendant, 42.9% of the cases were resentenced to life imprisonment, 25.7% were remanded to the trial court for resentencing, and 31.4% were sent back to the court of first instance (the trial court) for new trials.

Their conclusion was that white defendants are slightly more likely to receive a favorable decision than black defendants, and that defendants with male victims are slightly more likely to receive a favorable decision than defendants with female victims. The impact of the defendant's race, however, was found to be significantly modified by the victim's sex, and vice-versa. While 39.1% of the 23 convicted black defendants with female victims received a favorable decision, half of the 36 blacks convicted of killing a man received positive outcomes from the court. This pattern reverses with white defendants. Among the 36 appeals by defendants with female victims, 61.1% resulted in a favorable ruling, but 23 cases involving black defendants with female victims constituted the category least likely to receive a favorable decision. These findings overwhelmingly indicate the possibility remains that capital punishment is applied discriminatorily to this category of offense, and that the Florida Supreme Court is failing to correct the disparity of the trial courts in their decisions on direct appeal. In fact, Radelet and Vandiver argue the possibility that the Florida appeals court is reinforcing the biases against black defendants.

Gross and Mauro (1984, 1989) conducted a very extensive study of sentencing under post-**Furman** death penalty laws in Arkansas, Florida, Georgia, Illinois, Mississippi, North Carolina, Oklahoma, and Virginia. (See also Baldus et al., 1980a; Baldus et al., 1980b; Baldus, 1983; Baldus, 1985; Radelet and Pierce, 1985; Liebman, 1985; **McClesky v. Zant**, 1984; **McClesky v. Kemp**, 1987; Klepper et al., 1983; Thompson and Zimgraff, 1981; Vito and Keil, 1988; Hubbard, 1985; Smith, 1987; and compare Barnett, 1985; Heilburn, 1989.) While the data permitted separate analyses for Georgia, Florida, and Illinois, death sentences for the states of Arkansas, Mississippi, North Carolina, Oklahoma, and Virginia were analyzed collectively. In Georgia, Florida, and Illinois, Gross and Mauro (1984) found that while blacks and other racial minorities comprised the largest percentages of homicide victims over whites, the risk of a death sentence was far lower for those suspects charged with killing blacks in these three states than for those defendants charged with killing whites. For the state of Georgia, defendants who killed whites were almost ten times more likely to be sentenced to death than defendants whose victims blacks; in Florida, the killers of whites werer eight times more likely to be sentenced to death; and in Illinois, killers of whites were about six times more likely to be sentenced to death.

When controlling for the race of the victim, Gross and Mauro found that blacks who killed whites were far more likely to be sentenced to death than whites who killed whites. In Georgia, 20.1% of the death sentences were imposed on black defendants with white victims, and .8% of the homicides involving black defendants and black victims ended in death sentences. In Florida, 13.7% of the black-white category of defendant-victim were sentenced to death, while only .7% of the black defendant-victim category received the death sentence. In Illinois, 7.5% of the black defendants with white victims received the death penalty, and .6% of the blacks who killed other blacks were sentenced to death.

Gross and Mauro also found a consistent pattern of racial disparity in death sentencing in the states of Oklahoma, North Carolina, Virginia, Mississippi, and Arkansas. Due to the relatively small number of death sentences imposed in these states, imposition of death sentences within these five states were analyzed collectively. The most basic finding was that "in each state, the overall odds [log-odds] that an offender would receive the death penalty were much greater for killing a white victim than for killing a black victim" (1984:96).

MCCLESKY V. KEMP (1987)

In 1978, Warren McClesky, a black man, was convicted in Fulton County, Georgia of murdering a white police officer during an armed robbery of a furniture store. The conviction was in keeping with the Georgia statute, under which a jury cannot sentence a defendant to death for murder without a finding that the crime was aggravated by a least one of ten particular circumstances. McClesky failed to present any mitigating evidence to the jury and was subsequently sentenced to death.

On appeal to the U.S. Supreme Court, McClesky claimed that the Georgia capital sentencing process is administered in a racially discriminatory manner in violation of the eighth amendment protection against "cruel and unusual punishment," and that the discriminatory system violates the fourteenth amendment guarantee to the "equal protection of the law." McCleaky proffered the results of the Baldus et al. (1983) study in support of his claim. In 2,484 murder and non-negligent manslaughter cases in Georgia between 1973 and 1979, defendants who killed whites were sentenced to death in 11% of the cases, while defendants who killed blacks were sentenced to death in only 1% of the cases. Baldus et al. discovered that the death penalty was imposed in 22% of the cases where the defendant was convicted of murdering a white, 8% of the cases with white defendants and white victims, 3% of the cases with white defendants and black victims, and only 1% of the cases involving black defendants and black victims. Baldus et al. controlled for some 230 non-racial variables and found that none could account for the racial disparities in capital sentences among the different racial combinations of defendant-victim. Killers of whites were 4.3 times more likely to be sentenced to death than killers of blacks, and black defendants were 1.1 times more likely to be sentenced to death than other defendants.

McClesky claimed that race had, therefore, infected the administration of capital punishment in Georgia in two distinct ways. First, "prisoners who murder whites are more likely to be sentenced to death than prisoners who murder blacks," and, secondly, "black murderers are more likely to be sentenced to death than white murderers" (McClesky, 1987:9). McClesky held that he was discriminated against by the Georgia system of imposing the death penalty because he is a black man who killed a white.

On April 22, 1987, the U.S. Supreme Court handed down its decision. Associate Justice Powell delivered the opinion of the court and was joined by Chief Justice Rehnquist and Justices White, O'Connor, and Scalia. Justices Brennan, Blackmun, and Stevens filed dissenting opinions, with Justice Marshall joining in part. The question before the court in McClesky was "whether a complex statistical study that indicates a risk that racial consideration enters into capital sentencing determinations...is unconstitutional under the Eighth and Fourteenth Amendments" (McClesky, 1987:1).

Writing for the majority, Justice Powell held that the Baldus study does not prove that the administration of Georgia capital punishment system violates the equal protection clause of the fourteenth amendment or the eighth amendment's protection against cruel and unusual punishment. The court held that "a defendant who alleges an equal protection violation has the burden of proving 'the existence of purposeful discrimination,'" and that the "purposeful discrimination had a discriminatory effect on him". That is, McClesky must prove that they jury in his particular case acted with a discriminatory purpose; to establish only that a "pattern" of racial discrimination in imposing the death penalty to a select group of defendants is not sufficient to support a claim of constitutional violation of equal protection of the law. The court further held that McClesky's claim of cruel and unusual punishment also fails because McClesky "cannot prove a constitutional violation by demonstrating that other defendants who may be similarly situated did not receive the death penalty." The Georgia sentencing procedures were found by the court to be sufficient to focus discretion "on the particularized nature of the crime and the particularized characteristics of the individual defendant," and that it cannot, therefore, be presumed that McClesky's death sentence was "wantonly and freakishly" imposed.

The essence of the court's holding in **McClesky** is that there are acceptable standards of risk of racial discrimination in imposing the death penalty. The court held that the Baldus study simply shows that a discrepancy appears to correlate with race in imposing death sentences, but the "statistics do not prove that race enters into any capital sentencing decisions or that race was a factor in petitioners' cases." The court was also concerned that a finding for the defendant in this case would open other claims that "could be extended to other types of penalties and to claims based on unexplained discrepancies correlating to membership in other minority groups and even to gender."

To Justices Brennan, Marshall, Blackmun, and Stevens, "McClesky has clearly demonstrated that his death sentence was imposed in violation of the Eighth and Fourteenth Amendments," and that "[n]othing could convey more powerfully the intractable reality of the death penalty: 'that the effort to eliminate arbitrariiness in the infliction of that ultimate sanction is so plainly doomed to failure that it - and the death penalty - must be abandoned altogether" (**McClesky,** 1987:39). The dissenters argued that whether McClesky can prove racial discrimination in his particular case is totally irrelevant in evaluating his claim of a constitutional violation because the court has long recognized that to establish that a "pattern" of substantial risk of arbitrary and capricious capital sentencing suffices for a claim of unconstitutionality.

The dissenting justices also called into question the effectiveness of the statutory safeguards designed to curb discretionary use of the death penalty. Justice Brennan specifically argued that "[w]hile we may hope that a model of procedural fairness [as that established in **Gregg**] will curb the influence of race on sentencing, 'we cannot simply assume that the model works as intended; we must critique its performance in terms of its results'" (**McClesky,** 1987:19-20).

The dissenting justices were particularly dismayed by the court's fear that finding McClesky's claim sufficient would "open the door to widespread challenges to all aspects of criminal sentencing." To Justice Brennan, the court's rejection of McClesky's evidence of racial discrimination in imposition of the death penalty on the basis that it would open further challenges to criminal sentencing "is to ignore both the qualitatively different character of the death penalty and the particular repugnance of racial discrimination..." (**McClesky,** 1987:21-22).

CONCLUSIONS

This review has examined some of the more important studies that have been conducted on the extent to which arbitrariness and discrimination characterize the imposition of capital punishment in the United States. Two substantive issues have been discerned by this review. First, despite the attempts of the United States Supreme Court in **Furman v. Georgia** (1972) and **Gregg v. Georgia** (1976) to thwart racial discrimination in the use of capital punishment, the death penalty continues to be imposed against blacks in a "wanton" and "freakish" manner. Second, the specific finding by many of the studies that blacks who victimize whites consistently have the highest probability of receiving a capital sentence tends to substantiate the claim that capital punishment serves the extralegal function of majority group protection; namely, the death penalty acts to safeguard (through deterrence) that class of individuals (whites) who are least likely to be victimized.

The review has shown that the death penalty continues to be imposed to blacks in a capricious manner. That is, the evidence tends to confirm the hypothesis that arbitrariness is an inherent characteristic of the use of the death penalty. Studies by Reidel (1976) and Arkin (1980) show that the same degree of racial disparity present in pre-**Furman** cases is also present in post-**Furman** cases. Several other studies reviewed have also shown that the safeguards for guided discretion in the use of the death penalty have failed to correct for the racial disparities. Specific analyses have shown that as long as individual prosecutors continue to have broad based discretion in which cases they will try as capital cases in seeking the death penalty, racial discrimination in application of the death penalty will undoubtedly also. Racial discrimination in the use of the death penalty has also been found to be perpetuated through appellate review of capital cases. The irony here is that the appellate courts were highly touted in **Gregg** as the foremost safeguard against unguided discretion in the application of the death penalty.

Various studies reviewed in this chapter have shown that black defendants with white victims have been overwhelmingly convicted and sentenced to death when compared to other racial categories of defendant-victim. In the Wolfgang (1974) study, for example, race was found to be the only statistically significant variable that could account for the disproportionate application of the death penalty to blacks convicted of rape. Other empirical studies show that blacks convicted of raping a white woman comprise the most execution-prone offender group. Gross and Mauro (1984) have provided rather persuasive evidence that in several northern and southern states blacks who kill whites are highly more likely to be sentenced to death than any other racial combination of defendant-victim. These findings clearly show that when whites are the victims of heinous crimes perpetrated by blacks that the law is much more vehement in its punishment. The review clearly illustrated that racism has become so well entrenched and routinized in the imposition of the death penalty that it has developed into a systematic pattern of differential treatment of blacks that is specifically designed to protect members of the dominant white group. While a preponderance of contemporary authors and jurists writing on theories of crime and punishment readily denote retribution and deterrence as foremost rationales for imputing the death penalty to transgressors of heinous criminality, this review of empirical studies has shown that the death penalty serves the extralegal function of protecting whites.

As we have seen in reviewing post-**Gregg** studies, the wrong of racial prejudice, racial inequality, and caprice in the imposition of the death penalty have not been abolished by the procedural safeguards established in **Gregg**. Capital punishment continues to be imposed in a wanton and freakish and discriminatory manner against black criminal defeendants. As Goodman has explained, "the sentencer's choice between life and death increasingly appears inchoate and uncontrollable, a decision more visceral than cerebral" (1987:499). Empirically-based evidence that racial discrimination continues to influence the imposition of the death penalty has literally been ignored by the court in **McClesky**. The proposed safeguards that surround the application of the death penalty amount to no safeguards at all. The only substantive conclusion that can be drawn from this review is that the court has moved from a position of formally recognizing that imposition of the death penalty is imbued with racial prejudice (**Furman**), to a position of sanctioning racial prejudice as a cost of imposing the penalty (**McClesky**). It appears from the cases handed down from the court that racism is a legitimate penological doctrine. For the advocates of racial and ethnic equality, the death penalty cannot be morally justified on the premise that racial oppression, subjugation, and social subservience are legitimate liabilities of maintaining social order. Social order under these circumstances amounts to social order predicated upon racism.

CHAPTER THREE

AN EMPIRICAL ANALYSIS OF
RACIAL DISCRIMINATION IN THE IMPOSITION OF THE
DEATH PENALTY TO BLACKS

Imposition of the death penalty in the United States has been characterized by two movements. The first movement began during the 1830's and 1840's when executions were moved from town squares to prison courtyards. As such, executions were transformed from public events attracting thousands of people and a "carnival atmosphere" into a private and solemn affair attended principally by prison officials. Bowers explains that most states moved executions behind prison walls "partly for humane reasons," but also "to avoid the difficulty of controlling unruly mobs which became outraged at bungled hangings and last minute reprieves" (1974:31).

The transfer of authority from local communities to the power of the state to administrate executions characterizes the second movement in the imposition of capital punishment in the United States. With the advent of the state prison system and the concentration of penal authority with the state, Bowers (1974) points out that states began to require that executions be performed under state rather than local authority. Although the first state-imposed execution occurred as early as 1853 in the District of Columbia, the movement toward state-imposed executions was not readily adopted by the several states until the 1890's. Table 3-1 shows the number of executions (legal and illegal) in the United States by decades from the 1890's to the 1980's. While the table shows that the number of executions performed under local authority has decreased through the decades, the number of state-imposed exections has increased. Executions under local authority decreased from 87% of the total number of executions during the 1890's to accounting for no executions during the 1960's. In contrast, executions conducted under state authority increased from 13% of the total number of executions during the 1890's to accounting for all legally imposed executions at the present time. The percent decrease in locally authorized executions and the percent increase in state authorized executions has been about 12% per decade. Although illegal executions (lynchings) is fully discussed in Chapter 6, it is worth noting that lynchings have accounted for about 30.5% of the 12,212 executions performed in the United States between the 1890's and the 1980's.

Table 3-1

The Number of Persons Executed in the United States by Decade from
the 1890's to the 1980's

Years	State Authority*	Local Authority**	Illegal Executions***	Total
1890's	154	1,060	1,593	2,807
1900's	275	901	915	2,091
1910's	625	406	698	1,729
1920's	1,030	131	325	1,487
1930's	1,520	147	130	1,797
1940's	1,174	110	33	1,317
1950's	682	35	8	725
1960's	191	0	5	196
1970's	3****	0	0	3
1980's	58	0	1	59
Totals	5,712	2,790	3,708	12,212

*   Source: Teeters, N.K. and C.J. Zibulka. (1974). "Executions Under State Authority." In William J. Bowers' **Executions in America**. Lexington, MA: D.C. Heath and Company.

**   Source: Bowers, Willaim J. (1974). **Executions in America**. Lexington, MA: D.C. Heath and Company.

***   Source: The mean number of lynchings calculated from Cutler (1905), White (1969), Raper (1933), the United States Department of Commerce (Bureau of the Census - 1975), and Zangrando (1980).

**** Source: United States Department of Justice (Bureau of Justice Statistics). (1985). **Sourcebook**. Washington D.C.: United States Government Printing Office.

                 Reichel, Philip L. and Lisa Munden. (May, 1987). "Media Coverage of Executions." Unpublished manuscript. University of Northern Colorado. Presented at the 58th annual meeting of the Pacific Sociological Association in Eugene, Oregon.

THE TEETERS-ZIBULKA DATA

In 1968, Negley K. Teeters and Charles J. Zibulka compiled information on 5,708 state-imposed executions conducted between 1853 and 1967. The data set they created contains the names of the persons executed, the date of execution, the state of execution, the counties of prosecution, the criminal offense for which the prisoner was executed, the race and age of teh prisoner, and whether the prisoner was afforded an opportunity to appeal the capital case to a higher court prior to execution. All data other than appeal were supplied by wardens from the records of the Departments of Corrections of the various states. The data on appeals were derived from the **Decennial Digest** published by West Publishing Company (cited in Bowers, 1974:438). The Teeters-Zibulka inventory, therefore, provides a rich data source for empirically investigating the extent to which blacks have been disproportionately executed. These data contain invaluable information on 46.5% of all executions that have taken place in the United States between the 1890's and the 1960's.

Bowers (1975) has determined that the Teeters-Zibulka data are a virtually complete and exhaustive inventory of the executions performed in the United States under state authority. Bowers compared the information on executions from the Teeters-Zibulka inventory with official statistics on executions collected and published in aggregate form by the Federal Bureau of Prisons for the period between 1930 and 1970. The Bureau of Prisons statistics are comprised of the number of executions conducted annually within each state, the type of offense for which the person was executed, and the race of the offender for all executions performed during this time period. While the Teeters-Zibulka inventory lists some 3,567 executions performed under state authority since 1930, there were 3,859 executions reported by the Bureau of Prisons for the same time period. Bowers explains that the difference of 292 executions between thse two sources reflects the fact that Mississippi, Louisiana, Minnesota, Delaware, and Montana conducted executions under local authority for various periods since 1930. By simply subtracting the number of state imposed executions in each of these five states since 1930 in the Teeters-Zibulka data from the total number of civil executions reported by the Bureau of Prisons for each of these five states, Bowers found that there were only six executions unaccounted for by the Teeters-Zibulka data since 1930. These six executions amount to .01% of the total number of executions conducted under state authority since 1930.

THE REICHEL-MUNDEN DATA

We have supplemented the Teeters-Zibulka inventory with the Reichel-Munden inventory of 61 state-authorized executions in the United States from January 1977 to June 1986. These data were presented at the 58th Annual Meeting of the Pacific Sociological Association in Eugene, Oregon, in May of 1987. The unpublished paper that contains these data is entitled "Media Coverage of Executions" and was prepared by Professors Philip L. Reichel and Lisa Munden of the University of Northern Colorado at Boulder. These data contain the names of the prisoners executed, the state in which the execution was conducted, the method of execution (e.g., firing squad, electrocution, gas chamber, or lethal injection), the race of the prisoner executed, the age of the executed prisoner, and the date of the execution. These data are listed in Table 3-2. While these data **do not** contain information on the criminal offense for which the prisoner was executed and whether the prisoner was afforded appellate rview of the capital sentence prior to execution, recent United States Supreme Court decisions make it safe to assume that all prisoners executed during the period covered by the Reichel-Munden inventory were executed for murder and were afforded appellate review of their capital sentences. As was discussed in Chapter 2, the court held in **Coker v. Georgia** (1977) that imposition of the death penalty for the rape of an adult woman is "grossly disproportionate and excessive punishment" and therefore repugnant to the Eighth Amendment's prohibition against "cruel and unusual punishment." In addition, in **Gregg v. Georgia** (1976) the Court held that state capital sentencing statutes must entail appellate review of the sentence in order to insure that the death penalty is not applied in a discretionary manner. These data were compared with the number of executions published by the United States Department of Justice (Bureau of Justice Statistics, 1985) and no discrepancies between the two sources were discovered.

Table 3-2

Executions in the United States from January (1977) to June (1986)

Name	State	Method	Race	Age	Date
Gary Gilmore	UT	fr sq	white	36	1/17/77
John Spenkelink	FL	elec	white	30	5/25/79
Jessie Bishop	NV	gas	white	46	10/22/79
Stephan Judy	IN	elec	white	24	3/09/81
Frank Coppola	VA	elec	white	38	8/10/82
Charlie Brooks	TX	inj	black	40	12/07/82
John L. Evans	AL	elec	white	33	4/22/83
Jimmy L. Gray	MS	elec	white	34	9/01/83
Robert A. Sullivan	FL	elec	white	36	11/30/83
Robert W. Williams	LA	elec	black	53	12/14/83
John Elton Smith	GA	elec	white	30	12/15/83
Anthony Antone	FL	elec	white	66	1/26/84
Jonny D. Taylor	LA	elec	black	30	2/29/84
James D. Autry	TX	inj	white	29	3/14/84
James W. Hutchins	NC	inj	white	54	3/16/84
Ronald C. O'Bryan	TX	inj	white	39	3/31/84
Elmo P. Bonnier	LA	elec	white	35	4/05/84
Arthur F. Goode	FL	elec	white	30	4/05/84
James Adams	FL	elec	black	47	5/10/84
Carl Shriner	FL	elec	white	30	6/20/84
Ivon Stanley	GA	elec	black	28	7/12/84
David L. Washington	FL	elec	black	34	7/13/84
Earnest J. Dobbert	FL	elec	white	46	9/07/84
Timothy Haldwin	LA	elec	white	46	9/10/84
James D. Henry	FL	elec	black	34	9/20/84
Linwood Briley	VA	elec	black	30	10/12/84
Earnest Mnighton, Jr.	LA	elec	black	38	10/30/84
Thomas A. Barefoot	TX	inj	white	39	10/30/84
Velma Barfield*	NC	inj	white	52	11/02/84
Timothy Balmes	FL	elec	white	37	11/08/84
Alpha Otis Stephens	GA	elec	black	40	12/12/84
Robert Lee Willie	LA	elec	white	26	12/28/84

Table 3-2 (continued)

Name	State	Method	Race	Age	Date
David D. Martin	LA	elec	white	32	1/04/85
Roosevelt Green	GA	elec	black	28	1/09/85
Joseph C. Shaw	SC	elec	white	30	1/11/85
Doyle Skillern	TX	inj	white	49	1/16/85
James D. Kaulerson	FL	elec	white	34	1/30/85
Van Roosevelt Soloman	GA	elec	black	42	2/20/85
Jonny P. Witt	FL	elec	white	42	3/06/85
Stephan P. Morin	TX	inj	white	34	3/13/85
John Young	GA	elec	black	29	3/20/85
James D. Briley	VA	elec	black	28	4/18/85
Jesse De La Rosa	TX	inj	hisp	24	5/15/85
Marvin Francois	FL	elec	black	39	5/29/85
Charles Milton	TX	inj	black	34	6/25/85
Morris D. Mason	VA	elec	black	33	6/25/85
Henry M. Porter	TX	inj	hisp	43	7/09/85
Charles Rumbaugh	TX	inj	white	28	9/11/85
William Vandiver	IN	elec	black	37	10/16/85
Carroll Edward Cole	NV	inj	white	47	12/06/85
James Terry Roach	SC	elec	white	26	1/10/86
Charles Bass	TX	inj	white	30	3/12/86
Arthur L. Jones	AL	elec	black	47	3/21/86
Daniel Thomas	FL	elec	black	47	4/15/86
Jeffery Allen Barney	TX	inj	white	28	4/16/86
David L. Funchess	FL	elec	black	39	4/22/86
Jay K. Pinkerton	TX	inj	white	24	5/15/86
Ronald J. Straight	FL	elec	white	42	5/20/86
Rudy Ramos Esquivel	TX	inj	hisp	50	6/09/86
Kenneth Brock	TX	inj	white	37	6/19/86
Jerome Bowden	GA	elec	black	33	6/25/86

Source: Reichel, Philip L. and Lisa Munden. (May, 1987). "Media
         Coverage of Executions." Unpublished manuscript.
         University of Northern Colorado. Presented at the 58th
         annual meeting of the Pacific Sociological Association in
         Eugene, Oregon.

CHARACTERISTICS OF THE DATA

Tables 3-3 through 3-7 represent frequency distributions of the combined data sources contained within the Teeters-Zibulka and the Reichel-Munden inventories. The various tables show the number of executions by state, by year, by race, by offense, and by appeal. Table 3-3 specifically notes the number of executions per state for the periods in which each state conducted executions, and the period of abolition for each state. Table 3-3 also shows the variables for which there is missing data. There are no data on the number of state-imposed executions for Alaska, Delaware, Hawaii, Michigan, Montana, Rhode Island, Wisconsin, Michigan, Minnesota, and Wisconsin have had statewide abolition of the death penalty for the period covered by the Teeters-Zibulka and Reichel-Munden data. Delaware and Montana performed executions during the period covered by these inventories, but these executions were conducted under local authority and not state authority. Rhode Island has not conducted any executions, although the death penalty is still applicable to persons who kill while serving a life sentence. The table further shows that 14% of the data on the race[3] of the offender and 10% of the data on whether the offender had their capital case appealed[4] to a higher court prior to execution is missing.

Table 3-3

Executions Under State Authority for 42 states
and the District of Columbia

State	Period of Executions	Period of Abolition	Number of Executions	Missing Data
Alabama	1927-1986		152	
Arizona	1910-1963	1916-1918	63	
Arkansas	1913-1964		168	
California	1893-1967		502	Race=259
Colorado	1890-1967	1897-1901	77	Race=76
Conneticut	1884-1960		73	
D.C.	1853-1957	1973-	113	App=113
Florida	1924-1986		200	
Georgia	1924-1986		421	
Idaho	1901-1957		9	
Illinois	1928-1962		100	Race=64
Indiana	1897-1985		75	
Iowa	1894-1963	1965-1973	31	
Kansas	1944-1965		15	
Kentucky	1911-1962		170	
Louisiana	1957-1986		19	
Maine	1864-1885	1887-	7	
Maryland	1923-1961		79	
Massachusetts	1901-1947	1980-	65	Race=65
Mississippi	1955-1986		42	
Missouri	1938-1965		40	
Nebraska	1903-1959		20	
Nevada	1905-1986		35	Race=34
New Hampshire	1869-1939		12	Race=12
New Jersey	1907-1963		160	
New Mexico	1933-1960	1969-	8	Race=8
New York	1890-1963	1965-	696	Race=29
North Carolina	1910-1986		362	
North Dakota	1905	1915-1975	1	Race=1
Ohio	1885-1963		343	App=343
Oklahoma	1915-1966		83	
Oregon	1904-1962	1914-1920	59	Race=59
Pennsylvania	1915-1962	1914-1920	350	Race=104
South Carolina	1912-1962 1984-1986		242	
South Dakota	1947	1915-1939	1	Race=1
Tennessee	1916-1960		125	App=125
Texas	1924-1986		371	
Utah	1903-1977		32	Race=31
Vermont	1864-1954	1965-	21	Race=21
Virginia	1908-1986		240	
Washington	1904-1963	1913-1919	73	
West Virginia	1899-1959	1965	94	
Wyoming	1912-1965		14	Race=14

Table 3-4 shows the number of executions per decade from 1853 to 1986 as reported in the Teeters-Zibulka and Reichel-Munden inventories. The table shows that there has been a pattern of growth and decline in imposition of the death penalty under state authority during this period. A period of dormancy in applying the death penalty has occurred between 1853 and 1889 and accounts for less than 10% of all state-imposed executions. This period of executions accounts for less than a .1% increase in executions per decade. A period of rapid growth in imposing the penalty, however, began in the 1890's and reached a peak period during the 1930's. For the forty-year period between the 1890's and the 1920's there were an additional 2,087 executions, accounting for 36.4% of all executions performed during the entire period covered by the Teeters-Zibulka inventory. The percent increase during this period rose from 2.1% during the 1890's and the 1900's, to 6.1% during the 1900's and 1910's, to a percent increase of 7.1% during the 1910's and the 1920's. The peak period of executions in the United States occurred during the 1930's. During this period there were 1,520 executions that accounted for about 26.6% of all executions. The percent increase iin the number of executions fromo the 1920's to the 1930's was about 8.6%. A period of decline in the number of executions began during the 1940's; the number of executions declined from a high of 1,520 in the 1930's to a low of 191 during the 1960's. While the percent decrease rose from 6.1% from the 1930's to the 1940's, and to 8.5% from the 1940's to the 1950's, the largest percent devrease in the number of executions rose to 8.7% from the 1950's to the 1960's. It wasn't until the 1960's, however, that the number of state imposed executions fell to a low comparable to the number of executions conducted during the 1890's; less then 10% of the total number of executions per decade.

Table 3-4

Executions Under State Authority by Decades

Years	Number of Executions	Relative Percent
1853-1869	11	.2
1871-1879	17	.3
1880-1889	26	.4
1890-1899	155	2.7
1900-1909	277	4.8
1910-1919	626	10.9
1920-1929	1029	18.0
1930-1939	1520	26.3
1940-1949	1171	20.3
1950-1959	685	11.8
1960-1967	191	3.3
1970-1979	3	.0
1980-1986	58	1.0

Table 3-5 shows the number of persons executed from 1853 to 1986 according to the race of the person executed. Even with 14% (808) of the data missing on the race of the person executed, the table shows that racial disparity has occurred in imposing the death penalty to blacks when compared to non-blacks. While the number of non-blacks executed constituted 41.1% (2,278) of the total number of executions for which the race of the offender is known, blacks comprised 44.8% (2,588) of that total. The degree of racial disproportionality in imposing the death penalty becomes even more apparent when we consider their relative proportion of the American population. According to the United States Department of Commerce (Bureau of the Census, 1975), at no point between 1850 and 1970 has the black population of the United States exceeded an "average" of 11.2% of the entire American population. The census data show that blacks comprised a high of 15.6% of the total population during the 1850's, fell to a low of 9.6% during the 1930's and 1940's, and rose again to 11.0% in the 1970's. The point here is that while the black population of the United States has comprised an average of about 12% of the entire American population for the one hundred and twenty year period from the 1850's to the 1970's, black executions have constituted over half of all executions performed during that time period.

Table 3-5

The Number of Prisoners Executed Under States Authority
from 1853 to 1986 by Race

Race	Frequency	Relative Percent	Adjusted Percent
White	2278	39.4	45.8
Black	2588	44.8	52.2
Other	98	1.7	1.9
Missing	808	14.0	Missing
Total	5769	99.9*	99.9

* Percents do not add up to 100% due to rounding.

Table 3-6 shows that 88.5% (5,110) of all executions from 1853 to 1986 have been conducted for the crime of murder. While the crime of rape constitutes 9.7% of all executions, the crimes of robbery, kidnapping, burglary, assault, espionage, carnal knowledge (statutory rape) and unknown crimes have comprised about 1.9% of all executions.

Table 3-6

The Number of Prisoners Executed Under States Authority
from 1853 to 1986 by the Offense

Offense	Frequency	Relative Percent	Adjusted Percent
Murder	5110	88.5	88.9
Rape	552	9.7	9.7
Robbery	32	.6	.6
Kidnapping	20	.4	.4
Burglary	12	.2	.2
Assault	9	.2	.2
Espionage	2	.0	.0
Carnal Knowledge	1	.0	.0
Total	5769	100.0	100.0

Table 3-7 shows that of the total number of executions between 1853 and 1986, 3,674 (63.6%) capital cases were appealed to a higher (state and/or federal) court, while 1,515 (26.2%) cases were not appealed to higher courts before execution. The table also shows that for 580 (10.2%) of the executions it is unknown whether the capital case was appealed to a higher court prior to execution of the prisoner.

Table 3-7

The Number of Prisoners Executed Under States Authority
from 1853 to 1986 by the Appeal

Appeal	Frequency	Relative Percent	Adjusted Percent
Yes	3674	63.6	64.6
No	1515	26.2	35.4
Missing	580	10.2	Missing
Total	5769	100.0	100.0

The degree to which systematic racial discrimination has characterized the imposition of state authorized executions in the United States becomes readily apparent when the information provided by the Teeters-Zibulka and Reichel-Munden inventories on race is crosstabulated with the state in which the execution was conducted, with the offense for which the person was executed, and whether the executed person's capital case was appealed to a higher court before execution. That is, both the "racial" and "regional" characteristics of state-imposed executions surface quite clearly through this analysis. The regional characteristic of principal concern here is disproportionate application of the death penalty to blacks in the South. For our purposes, then, the states in which state authorized executions were conducted have been categorized according to whether the state is geographically located in the southern region of the United States. Alabama, Arkansas, Florida, Georgia, Louisiana, Mississippi, North Carolina, South Carolina, Tennessee, Texas, and Virginia constitute the southern states. All other states that have conducted state authorized executions listed within the Teeters-Zibulka and Reichel-Munden data have been coded as non-southern states.

METHOD OF DATA ANALYSIS

As noted, the degree to which racial discrimination has characterized the imposition of state authorized executions in the United States can readily be determined from the information provided by the Teeters-Zibulka and Reichel-Munden data by crosstabulating the race of the prisoner executed with the state and year in which the prisoner was executed, the offense for which the prisoner was executed, and whether the defendant had been afforded the opportunity to appeal the capital case to a higher court prior to execution. To evaluate all of the possible interactions among the variables (race, state, year, offense, and appeal) would be a tedious task because the tables have many cells and are very complex. Log-linear (logit) regression analysis can quickly untangle the information contained in a crosstabulation table. Log-linear regression reveals which associations between the several variables are most important by determining whether the various interactions are statistically significant. As Hedderson has pointed out, log-linear regression "state[s] very precisely how interactions among certain variables affect the likelihood that a subject will be in a particular category on another variable" (1987:145).

LOG-LINEAR ANALYSIS

Tables 3-8 through 3-16 represent the comparison of models of logit regressions for the likelihood that the person executed was non-black on the effects of the state of execution, the year of execution, the offense for which the prisoner was executed, and whether or not the defendant's capital case was appealed before execution. Table 3-8 shows the direct effects of state, year, offense, and appeal on the likelihood that the offender executed was white. The only statistics that are relevant at this stage of the model building process are the "chi-square statistic" and "the probability of the null hypothesis" statistics. A direct or interaction effect is only significant if the chi-square value is improved by at least 3.84 and the probability factor is below .05. Table 3-8 shows that the main or direct effects of state in which the prisoner was executed, the offense for which the prisoner was executed, and whether the prisoner was afforded the opportunity to appeal the capital case are significant because the chi-square values for each of these effects are above 3.84 and the probability factor for each effect is below .05. Specifically, the direct effect of **state** has a chi-square value of 585.13 with a probability of .000 with one degree of freedom, the effect of **offense** is significant with a chi-square value of 101.00 and .000 probability, and the direct effect of **appeal** is a statistically significant effect with 60.86 chi-square and .000 probability. The direct effect of **year**, however, is not statistically significant because the chi-square value is only .11 (below 3.84) and the probability factor is .740 (above .05).

Table 3-8

Direct Effects of State, Year, Offense, and Appeal
on the Likelihood that the Offender is White

Effect	Parameter Estimate	Standard Error	Chi-Square	Probability of the Null Hypotheis
Intercept	1.057	.144	53.66	.000
State	-1.801	.074	585.13	.000
Year	0.007	.023	.11	.740
Offense	1.536	.152	101.00	.000
Appeal	-0.636	.081	60.86	.000

Tables 3-9 through 3-15 show the tests for significance of the various interaction effects among the variables. Table 3-9 specifically shows that the interaction effect of **state** by **year** has a significant effect on the likelihood that the prisoner executed was non-black. The chi-square value is 46.93 and the probability is .000. Table 3-10 tests for statistical significance of the interaction between the **state** of execution and the **offense** for which the prisoner was executed. Table 3-10 shows that the interaction effect of these two variables is significant at the .003 level of confidence with a chi-square value of 8.44. Table 3-11 shows, however, that the **state** by **appeal** interaction is **not** statistically significant at the .05 level of confidence with a chi-square value of 3.80. Table 3-12 shows that the **year** by **offense** interaction is significant with a chi-square value of 4.14 and a probability factor of .041. Table 3-13 shows that the interaction between **year** and **appeal** is **not** statistically significant with a chi-square value of .17 and a probability factor of .679. Table 3-14 shows that the **appeal** by **offense** interaction is also not statistically significant with a chi-square value of 1.07 and a probability of .299. Table 3-15 shows the tests for the significance of the **state** by **year**, **state** by **offense**, and **year** by **offense** interaction simultaneously. The table shows that the **year** by **offense** interaction is not statistically significant and, therefore, this interaction is deleted from the model and further consideration. The chi-square value is .19 and the probability is .663.

Table 3-9

Interaction Effect of State by Year
on the Likelihood that the Offender is White

Effect	Parameter Estimate	Standard Error	Chi-Square	Probability of the Null Hypotheis
Intercept	1.811	.186	94.49	.000
State	-3.760	.298	158.35	.000
Year	-0.126	.030	17.20	.000
Offense	-1.537	.152	101.28	.000
Appeal	-0.622	.083	56.10	.000
State-Year	0.315	.046	46.93	.000

Table 3-10

Interaction Effect of State by Appeal
on the Likelihood that the Offender is White

Effect	Parameter Estimate	Standard Error	Chi-Square	Probability of the Null Hypotheis
Intercept	1.022	.145	49.70	.000
State	-1.716	.085	399.30	.000
Year	0.006	.023	.08	.770
Offense	-1.548	.153	101.97	.000
Appeal	-0.491	.110	19.60	.000
State-Appeal	-0.314	.161	3.80	.051

Table 3-11

Interaction Effect of State by Offense
on the Likelihood that the Offender is White

Effect	Parameter Estimate	Standard Error	Chi-Square	Probability of the Null Hypotheis
Intercept	1.054	.144	53.14	.000
State	-1.854	.076	581.19	.000
Year	0.011	.023	.24	.625
Offense	-2.317	.325	50.83	.000
Appeal	-0.618	.082	56.87	.000
State-Offense	1.062	.365	8.44	.003

Table 3-12

Interaction Effect of Year by Appeal
on the Likelihood that the Offender is White

Effect	Parameter Estimate	Standard Error	Chi-Square	Probability of the Null Hypotheis
Intercept	1.088	.163	44.44	.000
State	-1.802	.074	585.33	.000
Year	0.002	.026	.01	.917
Offense	-1.537	.152	101.12	.000
Appeal	-0.757	.303	6.22	.012
Year-Appeal	-0.021	.052	.17	.679

Table 3-13

Interaction Effect of Year by Offense
on the Likelihood that the Offender is White

Effect	Parameter Estimate	Standard Error	Chi-Square	Probability of the Null Hypotheis
Intercept	1.105	.146	56.84	.000
State	-1.800	.074	583.40	.000
Year	-7.400	.023	.00	.975
Offense	-3.133	.815	14.77	.000
Appeal	-0.629	.081	59.35	.000
Year-Offense	0.241	.118	4.14	.041

Table 3-14

Interaction Effect of Appeal by Offense
on the Likelihood that the Offender is White

Effect	Parameter Estimate	Standard Error	Chi- Square	Probability of the Null Hypotheis
Intercept	1.051	.144	52.94	.000
State	-1.806	.747	584.83	.000
Year	0.008	.023	.12	.727
Offense	-1.416	.187	57.11	.000
Appeal	-0.613	.084	52.88	.000
Appeal-Offense	-0.334	.323	1.07	.299

Table 3-15

Interaction Effect of Appeal-Offense and State-Offense
on the Likelihood that the Offender is White

Effect	Parameter Estimate	Standard Error	Chi- Square	Probability of the Null Hypotheis
Intercept	1.808	.187	92.98	.000
State	-3.753	.302	153.51	.000
Year	-0.123	.030	16.04	.000
Offense	-2.567	.793	10.48	.001
Appeal	-0.604	.083	52.35	.000
State-Offense	0.927	.379	5.98	.014
Year-Offense	0.051	.118	.19	.663

FINDINGS

Table 3-15 represents the parameter estimates[5] of the preferred model of direct and interaction effects on the likelihood that the prisoner executed was non-black. While Table 3-8 shows that the direct effects of the **state** of execution, the **offense** for which the prisoner was executed, and whether the executed prisoner was afforded appellate opportunity of the capital case are significant direct effects that are contained in the preferred model, Table 3-15 shows further that the interaction effects of **state** by **offense** and **state** by **year** are significant interaction effects that are also contained in the preferred model.

STATE

The parameter estimate for the direct effect of the **state** in which the prisoner was executed on the likelihood that the prisoner was black is 1.801. This parameter estimate means that the likelihood that the prisoner was black and executed in a southern state is increased by 1.801 log-odds over the likelihood that white prisoners were executed in southern states. That is, the likelihood that blacks were executed in the southern states is considerably greater (1.801 log-odds greater) than the likelihood that whites were executed in southern states.

OFFENSE

The parameter estimate for the direct effect of the **offense** for which the prisoner was executed on the likelihood that the probability that the prisoner was white is -1.536. This estimate means that the likelihood that white prisoners were executed for rape is decreased by 1.536 log-odds over the likelihood that blacks were executed for rape. That is, there is a 1.536 log-odds increase in the likelihood that black prisoners were executed for the crime of rape when compared to white prisoners.

APPEAL

The parameter estimate for the direct effect of whether the prisoner was afforded the opportunity to **appeal** the capital case to a higher court prior to execution on the likelihood that the prisoner was white is -.636. This parameter estimate basically shows that the likelihood that white prisoners were not afforded an appeal prior to execution is decreased by .636 log-odds over the likelihood that blacks prisoners were not afforded an appeal prior to execution. That is, black prisoners were less likely than white prisoners to be afforded an appeal prior to execution.

STATE/YEAR INTERACTION

The parameter estimate for the **state** by **year** interaction is .310. This interaction effect means that the likelihood that white prisoners were executed in non-southern states during the later years covered by the Teeters-Zibulka and Reichel-Munden data is increased by .310 log-odds over the likelihood that black prisoners were executed in non-southern states during later years. In other words, as executions became more prevalent the likelihood that blacks were executed in the southern states was increased.

STATE/OFFENSE INTERACTION

The parameter estimate for the **state** by **offense** interaction is -.969. This interaction effect shows that the likelihood that white prisoners were executed in southern states for the crime of rape decreases by .969 log-odds over the likelihood that blacks pripsoners were executed in southern states for rape.

INTERPRETATION OF THE ANALYSIS

Several important findings concerning the manner in which the death penalty has been applied to blacks have been revealed by our analysis. First, our analysis has shown that black prisoners have been considerably more likely to have been executed in Southern states than white prisoners. Secondly, our analysis has shown that black prisoners have had a greater likelihood of being executed for rape than white prisoners. Thirdly, black prisoners have been less likely to have been afforded the opportunity to appeal their capital cases to a higher court than white prisoners. Fourthly, black prisoners were more likely to have been executed in later years than in the earlier years covered by the Teeters-Zibulka and Reichel-Munden inventories. Finally, the findings of our analysis show that black prisoners were more likely to have been executed for the crime of rape in Southern states than white prisoners. Taken together, these various findings provide rather persuasive evidence that black prisoners have been subjected to a systematic pattern of racial discrimination in the imposition of the death penalty.

Secondly, the regional characteristic of racial discrimination in imposing the death penalty to blacks is illustrated very clearly by the finding that the likelihood that the prisoner executed was white and executed in a Southern state is considerably decreased over the likelihood that blacks were executed in Southern states. This finding supports the conclusion of a number of other studies.[6] This is not to argue, however, that racial discrimination is absent from imposing the death penalty in Northern states.[7] The most significant aspect of the immediate finding taken in conjunction with previous research findings is that a racist ideology underscores and influences the use of the death penalty. While the racist ideology may be more pronounced in the South, it must be recognized that the broad based racial prejudice and racial discrimination that accompany the racist ideology are not limited to the South.

The extent to which the imposition of the death penalty has been characterized by racial discrimination is overwhelmingly illustrated by the finding that the likelihood that white prisoners have been executed for rape dramatically decreases over the likelihood that black prisoners were executed for the crime of rape. This finding means that the likelihood is greater that black prisoners were executed for rape than white prisoners. This particular finding, however, must also be considered in light of previous research that has been conducted on racial disparity in application of the death penalty in order to gain insight into the sociological significance of this finding.

Studies by the Florida Civil Liberties Union (1964), Wolfgang (1974), and Wolfgang and Reidel (1975) have shown that blacks convicted of raping a white woman have constituted that defendant-victim category that has suffered the highest execution rates than any other racial combination of defendant and victim. The study conducted by the Florida Civil Liberties Union (1964) found that 54% of all prisoners convicted of rape in Florida between 1940 and 1964 were black prisoners who had been convicted of raping a white woman, while white prisoners convicted of raping a white woman comprised only 5% of that total number of convictions. Moreover, none of the whites convicted of raping a black woman were sentenced to death. (See also Zangrando, 1980.) Likewise, the Wolfgang (1974) and Wolfgang and Reidel (1975) studies have shown that in several counties of eleven southern states between 1945 and 1965 black prisoners who were convicted of raping a white woman were eighteen times more likely to be sentenced to death than prisoners convicted of rape in any other racial combination of defendant and victim. In light of this previous research, then, it is safe to assume that an added dimension of the finding that black prisoners were more likely to have been executed for the crime of rape is that the vast majority of these prisoners have been executed for the rape of white woman. As Bowers has pointed out, "it follows that 90% of the blacks executed for rape had white victims, [and] that 85% of all executions for rape involved this offender-victim combination" (1974:78-79). It is equally safe to assume that none of the white prisoners were executed for the rape of a black woman.

Taken together, the finding of our analysis that black prisoners are more likely to have been executed for rape were executed for the rape of a white woman amounts to rather conclusive evidence that the death penalty has been particularly targeted against blacks who have raped white women. That is, black prisoners have been especially victimized by a systematic pattern of racial discrimination that had been particularly designed to protect the chastity of white women. From this standpoint, then, the death penalty amounts to an effective means by which the dominant white group can protect its interest. By invoking the threat of death, the white dominant group has been able to manipulate and control the social relations between black men and white women, while at the same time preserving without impunity white male superiority over black women. (See Marable, 1984; White, 1984.)

Both the racial and the regional aspects of racial discrimination in the imposition of the death penalty become even more clear from the finding that there is a statistically significant relationship between the race of the prisoner executed, the state in which the prisoner was executed, and the offense for which the prisoner was executed. The **state** by **offense** interaction effect on the likelihood that the prisoner executed was black specifically shows that black prisoners were considerably more likely to have been executed in Southern states for the crime of rape than were white prisoners. While the underlying rationale for the execution of black prisoners who raped white women was to restrict interracial contact between black men and white women in the South, it was actually fear by whites that blacks were becoming a rival economic, political, and social force in the South that was the primary motivation behind such a phenomenon as that of the rape myth. (See Zangrando, 1980.) The rape myth was simply a manifestation of this fear.

White (1929) explains that prior to the 1830's the alleged propensity for sex crimes against white women by black men was unprecedented in the South. That is, charges of raping a white woman against a black man were virtually nonexistent between 1619, when slavery was implemented as a labor force in the South, and 1830. This is not to argue that the opportunity for such crimes did not exist. White points out that given the large population of black slaves during this period that there was ample opportunity for such crimes to take place. The rape myth, therefore, amounts to nothing more than an illegitimate rationale for the white dominant group to justify its control over blacks. As Bowers writes, "(p)erhaps, to the dominant white majority under a caste-like system of relations between the races, this kind of rape is perceived as a challenge, at least symbolically, to its ability to regulate social order. In effect, the readiness to execute for black offender-white victim rape dramatizes the fact that it is not rape per se that the threat that a particular form of rape poses to established standards of separation and social distance between the races that make it a grave offense against the caste system itself" (1974:79).

The increased use of the death penalty as a mechanism of social control of blacks in the South is further illustrated by our finding that as executions became more prevalent, the likelihood that blacks were executed in Southern states dramatically increases over the likelihood that whites were executed in the South. The interaction effect between the **year** of execution and the **state** in which the execution was conducted on the likelihood that the race of the prisoner executed was black specifically shows that the likelihood that white prisoners were executed in non-southern states during the later years covered by the Teeters-Zibulka and Reichel-Munden inventories is increased significantly over the likelihood that black prisoners were executed in non-southern states during later years. This finding basically shows that there has been considerable variation within the categories of race and region over time. As was noted earlier, there has been a pattern of growth and decline in the imposition of the death penalty under state authority. During the period of dormancy (1853-1889), blacks comprised about 82% of the total number of executions in the South, and about 29% of the total number of executions in the non-southern states. From 1930 to 1939, the peak years of executions in the United States, blacks constituted about 74% of the total number of executions in the South, and approximately 27% of the total number of executions in the non-southern states. Even during the period of decline in the use of the death penalty from 1940 to the present day, blacks have comprised about 74% of the total number of executions in the southern states, and about 39% of the total number of executions in non-southern states.

The finding that there have been substantial regional differences in the use of the death penalty against blacks over time tends to support the claim that blacks became increasingly vulnerable to the penalty as a mechanism for social control. Bowers (1974) explains that the Civil War and Reconstruction disrupted racial segregation as a way of life in the South that had become well entrenched with the development of a plantation economy. In reacting to these types of disruptions in the racial segregated life styles of the South, "the white majority had displayed intense hostility toward the black minority and taken oppressive actions [e.g., executions] to regain and reaffirm its position of dominance in southern society" (Bowers, 1974:83).

The finding that the likelihood that white prisoners have not been afforded an appeal prior to execution is decreased over the likelihood that blacks have not been afforded an appeal tends to substantiate the claim that racial discrimination has not been strictly a southern phenomenon. The finding specifically shows that the effect of whether the prisoner was afforded the opportunity to appeal the capital case to a higher court prior to execution on the likelihood that the prisoner was white decreases significantly over the likelihood that blacks have not been afforded such an opportunity. However, it must be understood that the effect of appeal does not significantly (statistically) interact with the state of execution, the year of execution, or the offense for which the prisoner was executed. This lack of interaction between these variables means that there are no regional, temporal, or type of offense for which the prisoner was executed. This lack of interaction between these variables means that there are no regional, temporal, or type of offense variations to the finding that black prisoners have not been afforded the opportunity to appeal their capital cases. That is, blacks have been systematically denied the opportunity to appeal their capital cases notwithstanding the crime for which they were executed, the state in which they were executed, or the year in which they were executed. This evidence tends to indicate that lack of appellate review can be viewed as a national case of systematic racial discrimination against blacks in the imposition of the death penalty rather than simply a regional problem restricted to the South.

That our analysis has not revealed any regional, temporal, or type of offense variations in the finding that blacks have been systematically denied appellate review of their capital cases also tends to refute Bowers' claim that appeals prior to execution "refect judicial practices rather than the social backgrounds and personal characteristics of the condemned" (1974:61). Bowers contends that there was a rise in appeals among executed capital offenders in the South during the growth period in state-imposed executions and that this rise may have been another step in the process of "delocalization" of executions from local authority to the authority of the state. In addition, Bowers points out that appeals to federal district, circuit, and supreme courts were seldom made prior to the period of decline in state-imposed executions. The problem with this observation, however, is that if these judicial practices had any statistically significant impact on the regional, temporal, and type of offense variation on the likelihood that black prisoners were more or less likely to have been afforded appellate review of their capital cases, these interaction effects would certainly have been determined to be statistically relevant interaction effects by the log-linear regression analysis. The point is that changes in the judicial system due to historical development have not had a significant impact on racial discrimination in the imposition of the death penalty by eliminating racial disparity in appellate review of capital cases. In other words, the results of our empirical analysis show that any increase in the rate of appeals for capital offenders has not significantly altered the systematic pattern of racial discrimination in imposing the death penalty to blacks.

CONCLUSIONS

The purpose of this chapter has been to explore the issue of institutionalized racial discrimination in the application of the death penalty to black prisoners. Instatutionalized racial discrimination has been defined by Feagin (1984:16) as "organizationally prescribed...actions which by intention have a differential and negative impact on members of race and ethnic groups." The analysis presented in this chapter has presented rather conclusive evidence that the death penalty has been intentionally imposed on blacks as a mechanism by which to invoke both a differential (racial disparity) and negative (death) impact on blacks. That is, the death penalty has been used by the white dominant group as a means of controlling and regulating the social environment of blacks. The motivation of the white dominant group's action in using the death penalty in this manner has been to exploit and subordinate blacks to a subservient social position that they (blacks) occupied prior to Reconstruction. That is, the dominant white group has attempted to secure its economic, political, and social dominance over blacks by keeping blacks relegated to the powers of the white dominant group. The justification for white dominance has been the racist ideology of superiority.

Most empirically based research on the discriminatory and discretionary application of the death penalty to blacks has focused on particular regions of the country during a particular period in the historical development of capital punnishment. Our analysis, however, has utilized national execution data for the entire period in which legal executions came under the exclusive authority of states. The most substantive observation that can be made from our analysis is that blacks have been subjected to systematic racial discrimination throughout most of the United States and throughout the entire history of the imposition of capital punishment in this country. Our analysis shows that the likelihood that black prisoners were executed in southern states is considerably greater than the likelihood that white prisoners were executed in southern states; that the likelihood is greater that black prisoners were executed for rape; and that black prisoners were less likely to have been afforded appellate review of their capital cases. Our analysis further shows that black prisoners were dramtically more likely to have been executed in southern states for the crime of rape, and that as capital punishment became more prevalent within the criminal justice system that black prisoners were more likely to have been executed in the southern states than in non-southern states.

PART II

**RACIAL PREJUDICE AND THE DEATH PENALTY:
THE ROLE OF SOCIO-CULTURAL KNOWLEDGE**

CHAPTER FOUR

THE SOCIO-CULTURAL DIMENSION OF CAPITAL PUNISHMENT: LYNCHING AS A SOCIAL CONTROL MECHANISM

The importance of studying illegal executions (lynchings)[8] in the United States rests in the history that surrounds the lynching of Black persons. Statistics on lynchings from 1882 to 1970 indicate that lynching has been both a **racial** and **regional** phenomenon. The lynching of Black persons constitutes about three-fourths of all lynchings, and those states with the largest percentages of black lynchings are geographically located in the South. In addition, data on lynchings show that blacks have been disproportionately lynched for murder, rape, and a number of minor crimes. In particular, most of the lynching offenses for blacks were specifically designed to restrict contact between black men and white women (Marable, 1984). No such crimes, however, were directed toward defining the degree of social tolerance between black women and white men.

The lynching of blacks has also involved a beastiality "unknown to even the most uncivilized parts of the world." Men, women, and children have been fiendishly tortured before death and many had their bodies barbarically mutilated after death. Further, the extent to which black lynchings were sanctioned by the general public is illustrated by the fact that black lynchings were almost always accompanied by public fanfare and circus like jubilance. Pro-lynching sentiment took on an aire of political approval with the silent acquiescence of court officials toward the violent lynching of blacks.

Comparison between legal and illegal (lynchings) executions tends to show that the locus of authority to impose executions simply transferred from the hands of the lynch mob to the power of the State. Such a comparison also shows that executions have been imposed on blacks in a discretionary and discriminatory manner. The underlying rationale for black lynchings has been to maintain social control of blacks by invoking morbid terror. Fear that blacks would become a social, political, and economic force in the United States moved whites to manifest a hatred for blacks. For purposes here, the legal and illegal execution of blacks can be viewed as a mechanism by which the white dominant gorup of American society has attempted to relegate blacks to a subjugated and subservient social position to that of whites.

RACIAL DISPROPORTIONALITY OF LYNCHINGS

Several researchers have compiled historically based data on the number of persons lynched in the United States. A major problem with these sources, however, is that they all report different findings for the number of persons lynched per year according to race. The inaccurate reporting of lynching is due in part to inadequate methods of maintaining official records.

The earliest study of lynchings in the United States was conducted by James Elbert Cutler in 1905. Cutler obtained data on the number of persons lynched from 1882 to 1903 from annual reviews of disasters and crimes in the United States published by the **Chicago Tribune**. From these yearly itemized summaries, Cutler was able to learn the date of the lynching, the name of the person lynched, the victim's color (race) and nationality, the alleged crime for which the victim was lynched, and the town and state where the lynching took place. Cutler was able to correct for any discrepancies in the data by comparing these findings to similar reports that had been published during the same period in the **New York Times** and the **New York Tribune**.

Cutler's data have been reproduced in Table 4-1. The table reveals that between the years 1882 and 1903, 3,337 persons were lynched in the United States. Of this number, 2,060 (61.7%) were black, 1,169 (35.0%) were white, and 108 (3.2%) were racially categorized as others. This last category consisted of 45 (1.3%) Indians, 28 (.8%) Italians, 20 (.5%) Mexicans, 12 (.3%) Chinese, 1 (.02%) Japanese, 1 (.02%) Swiss, and 1 (.02%) Bohemian. Cutler also reported that 63 (1.8%) of the 3,337 persons lynched between 1882 and 1903 were women; 40 blacks and 23 whites.

Table 4-1

The Number of Persons Lynched in the United States from 1882 to 1903

Year	White	Black	Other	Total
1882	66	46	2	114
1883	75	47	12	134
1884	149	52	10	211
1885	103	74	7	184
1886	62	74	2	138
1887	50	71	1	122
1888	69	70	3	142
1889	80	95	1	176
1890	34	88	6	128
1891	56	124	15	195
1892	74	156	5	235
1893	35	155	10	200
1894	61	132	4	197
1895	62	109	9	180
1896	47	80	4	131
1897	36	123	6	165
1898	25	100	2	127
1899	18	84	5	107
1900	10	105	0	115
1901	27	106	2	135
1902	9	87	1	97
1903	18	84	2	104
Total	1169	2060	108	3337

Source: Cutler, James Elbert. (1905:170b). **Lynch-Law: An Investigation into the History of Lynching in the United States.** New York: Longsman, Green and Company.

Note: Cutler did not tabulate these date. The data are taken from a graph that Cutler constructed of the data.

In 1929, Walter White published findings on the number of persons lynched in the United States between 1882 and 1929. The figures for the years up to and including 1903 were taken from Cutler's (1905) study. White used two data sources for compiling the number of lynchings that had occurred between 1904 and 1927. One source was a statistical study originally published in 1919 by the National Association for the Advancement of Colored People (NAACP) entitled, **Thirty Years of Lynchings in the United States.** These data were compiled from records of lynchings that had been kept by the **Chicago Tribune**, the Tuskegee Institute and, since 1912, from an annual summary of the number of persons lynched for the thirty-year period from 1889 to 1918. The findings were compared with figures on lynchings prepared by Monroe N. Work of the Tuskegee Institute and published in the **World Almanac** (1927). A problem with White's data, however, is that he combined the 108 persons classified as "others" by Cutler with the number of white persons lynched. White, therefore, began his count of the number of white persons lynched with 1,227, rather than the 1,169 reported by Cutler. Table 4-2 shows the data reported by White. According to White, there were an additional 1,614 persons lynched in the United States between 1904 and 1927. There were 161 (9.9%) whites and 1,453 (90.1%) blacks lynched during this period.

Table 4-2

The Number of Persons Lynched in the United States from 1904 to 1927

Year	White	Black	Other	Total
1904	7	79	-	86
1905	5	60	-	65
1906	4	64	-	68
1907	3	59	-	62
1908	8	92	-	100
1909	14	75	-	89
1910	10	80	-	90
1911	8	72	-	80
1912	3	86	-	89
1913	1	85	-	86
1914	5	69	-	74
1915	46	99	-	145
1916	7	65	-	72
1917	2	52	-	54
1918	4	63	-	67
1919	4	79	-	83
1920	8	57	-	65
1921	6	58	-	64
1922	7	54	-	61
1923	2	26	-	28
1924	0	16	-	16
1925	0	18	-	18
1926	5	29	-	34
1927	2	16	-	18
Total	161	1453	-	1614

Source: White, Walter. (1929:231-232). Rope and Faggot.
          New York: Arno Press and the New York Times.

William Raper (1933) secured data on the number of persons lynched between 1889 and 1932 from **The Negro Year Book: An Annual Encyclopedia of the Negro, 1931-1932**, and from materials he obtained from the Department of Records and Research at the Tuskegee Institute. Raper's data have been reproduced in Table 4-3. There is a severe discrepancy between White (1929) and Raper's (1933) data on the number of persons lynched across racial categories and the total number of persons lynched. For example, for 1915, White's data (Table 4-2) show that there were 46 whites and 99 blacks lynched, whereas Raper's (Table 4-3) data show that there were 13 whites and 54 blacks lynched. Despite this difference, both sources clearly illustrate a comparable degree of disproportionality between the number of blacks and the number of whites lynched. Raper's data show that between the years 1889 and 1932, there was a total of 3,745 persons lynched - 791 (21.1%) whites and 2,954 (78.8%) blacks.

Table 4-3

The Number of Persons Lynched in the United States from 1889 to 1932

Year	White	Black	Other	Total
1889	81	95	-	176
1890	37	90	-	127
1891	71	121	-	192
1892	100	155	-	255
1893	46	155	-	201
1894	56	134	-	190
1895	59	112	-	171
1896	51	80	-	131
1897	44	122	-	166
1898	25	102	-	127
1899	23	84	-	107
1900	8	107	-	115
1901	28	107	-	135
1902	11	86	-	97
1903	17	86	-	103
1904	4	83	-	87
1905	5	61	-	66
1906	8	65	-	73
1907	3	60	-	63
1908	7	93	-	100
1909	14	73	-	87
1910	9	65	-	74
1911	8	63	-	71
1912	4	61	-	65
1913	1	50	-	51
1914	3	49	-	52
1915	13	54	-	67
1916	4	50	-	54
1917	2	36	-	38
1918	4	60	-	64
1919	7	76	-	83
1920	8	53	-	61
1921	5	59	-	64
1922	6	51	-	57
1923	4	29	-	33
1924	0	16	-	16
1925	0	17	-	17
1926	7	23	-	30
1927	0	16	-	16
1928	1	10	-	11
1929	3	7	-	10
1930	1	20	-	21
1931	1	12	-	13
1932	2	6	-	8
Total	791	2954	-	3745

Source: Raper, Arthur F. (1933:480-481). The Tragedy of Lynching.
           Chapel Hill: The University of North Carolina.

Two other sources on the number of lynchings in the United States have been published by the United States Department of Commerce (1975) and by Robert L. Zangrando (1980). Both sources have been reproduced in Table 4-4 and Table 4-5, respectively. By contrasting the data in these two tales, it can be noted that both data sources show approximately the same number of persons lynched across racial categories for the same years. Zangrando obtained his statistical information on the number of lychings in the United States from the Archieves at the Tuskegee Institute in February of 1979. The United States Department of Commerce, however, has made no reference as to the source of its data. Table 4-4 shows that the United States Department of Commerce reports 4,745 persons lynched between 1882 and 1970. Of those persons lynched, 1,296 (27.3%) were white and 3,449 (72.6%) were blacks. Table 4-5 shows that Zangrando reports 1,297 (27.3%) whites and 3,445 (72.6%) blacks lynched between 1882 and 1968 - comprising a total of 4,742 persons. Both data sources show that there were no persons lynched between 1952 and 1954, in 1956, in 1958, in 1960, and between 1965 and 1970.

Table 4-4

The Number of Persons Lynched in the United States from 1882 to 1970

Year	White	Black	Other	Total
1882	64	49	-	113
1883	77	53	-	130
1884	160	51	-	211
1885	110	74	-	184
1886	64	74	-	138
1887	50	70	-	120
1888	68	69	-	137
1889	76	94	-	170
1890	11	85	-	96
1891	71	113	-	184
1892	69	161	-	230
1893	34	118	-	152
1894	58	134	-	192
1895	66	113	-	179
1896	45	78	-	123
1897	35	123	-	158
1898	19	101	-	120
1899	21	85	-	106
1900	9	106	-	115
1901	25	105	-	130
1902	7	85	-	92
1903	15	84	-	99
1904	7	76	-	83
1905	5	57	-	62
1906	3	62	-	65
1907	3	58	-	61
1908	8	89	-	97
1909	13	69	-	82
1910	9	67	-	76
1911	7	60	-	67
1912	2	62	-	64
1913	1	51	-	52
1914	4	51	-	55
1915	13	56	-	69
1916	4	50	-	54
1917	2	36	-	38
1918	4	60	-	64
1919	7	76	-	83
1920	8	53	-	61
1921	5	59	-	64
1922	6	51	-	57
1923	4	29	-	33
1924	0	16	-	16
1925	0	17	-	17
1926	7	23	-	30
1927	0	16	-	16
1928	1	10	-	11

Table 4 (continued)

Year	White	Black	Other	Total
1929	3	7	-	10
1930	1	20	-	21
1931	1	12	-	13
1932	2	6	-	8
1933	4	24	-	28
1934	0	15	-	15
1935	2	18	-	20
1936	0	8	-	8
1937	0	8	-	8
1938	0	6	-	6
1939	1	2	-	3
1940	1	4	-	5
1941	0	4	-	4
1942	0	6	-	6
1943	0	3	-	3
1944	0	2	-	2
1945	0	1	-	1
1946	0	6	-	6
1947	0	1	-	1
1948	1	1	-	2
1949	0	3	-	3
1950	1	1	-	2
1951	0	1	-	1
1952	0	0	-	0
1953	0	0	-	0
1954	0	0	-	0
1955	0	3	-	3
1956	0	0	-	0
1957	1	0	-	1
1958	0	0	-	0
1959	0	1	-	1
1960	0	0	-	0
1961	0	1	-	1
1962	0	0	-	0
1963	0	1	-	1
1964	2	1	-	3
Total	1296	3449	-	4745

Source: United States Department of Commerce (Bureau of the Census).
           Washington D.C.: United States Government Printing Office.
           September, 1975.

Note: There were no lynchings recorded from 1965 to 1970.

Table 4-5

The Number of Persons Lynched in the United States from 1882 to 1968

Year	White	Black	Other	Total
1882	64	46	-	113
1883	77	53	-	130
1884	160	51	-	211
1885	110	74	-	184
1886	64	74	-	138
1887	50	70	-	120
1888	68	69	-	137
1889	76	94	-	170
1890	11	85	-	96
1891	71	113	-	184
1892	69	161	-	230
1893	34	118	-	152
1894	58	134	-	192
1895	66	113	-	179
1896	45	78	-	123
1897	35	123	-	158
1898	19	101	-	120
1899	21	85	-	106
1900	9	106	-	115
1901	25	105	-	130
1902	7	85	-	92
1903	15	84	-	99
1904	7	76	-	83
1905	5	57	-	62
1906	3	62	-	65
1907	3	58	-	61
1908	8	89	-	97
1909	13	69	-	82
1910	9	67	-	76
1911	7	60	-	67
1912	2	62	-	64
1913	1	51	-	52
1914	4	51	-	55
1915	13	56	-	69
1916	4	50	-	54
1917	2	36	-	38
1918	4	60	-	64
1919	7	76	-	83
1920	8	53	-	61
1921	5	59	-	64
1922	6	51	-	57
1923	4	29	-	33
1924	0	16	-	16
1925	0	17	-	17
1926	7	23	-	30
1927	0	16	-	16
1928	1	10	-	11

Table 4-5 (continued)

Year	White	Black	Other	Total
1929	3	7	-	10
1930	1	20	-	21
1931	1	12	-	13
1932	2	6	-	8
1933	4	24	-	28
1934	0	15	-	15
1935	2	18	-	20
1936	0	8	-	8
1937	0	8	-	8
1938	0	6	-	6
1939	1	2	-	3
1940	1	4	-	5
1941	0	4	-	4
1942	0	6	-	6
1943	0	3	-	3
1944	0	2	-	2
1945	0	1	-	1
1946	0	6	-	6
1947	0	1	-	1
1948	1	1	-	2
1949	0	3	-	3
1950	1	1	-	2
1951	0	1	-	1
1952	0	0	-	0
1953	0	0	-	0
1954	0	0	-	0
1955	0	3	-	3
1956	0	0	-	0
1957	1	0	-	1
1958	0	0	-	0
1959	0	1	-	1
1960	0	0	-	0
1961	0	1	-	1
1962	0	0	-	0
1963	0	1	-	1
1964	2	1	-	3
Total	1297	3445	-	4742

Source: Zangrando, Robert L. (1980). The NAACP Crusade Against Lynching, 1909-1950. Philadelphia: Temple University Press.

Note: There were no lynchings recorded between 1965 and 1968.

In an effort to reconcile the differences in the number of black and white lynchings reported by the several data sources discussed above, the statistical mean of both blacks and whites lynched per year was calculated from those data sourcees. A summary of the mean number of lynchings are contained in Table 4-6. The Cutler (1905), Zangrando (1980), and the United States Department of Commerce (1979) data were used to calculate the means for the number of blacks and whites lynched in the United States between 1882 and 1888. For the years 1889 to 1903, the Cutler, Zangrando, Raper (1933), and the United States Department of Commerce data were used. To calculate the means for the number of blacks and whites lynched between 1904 and 1918, the White (1929) data were used along with that provided by Zangrando, Raper, and the United States Department of Commerce. Between 1919 and 1927, the means were determined by using data from the White, Zangrando, Raper, and the United States Department of Commerce reports. For the years 1928 to 1932, Zangrando, Raper, and the United States Department of Commerce data provided the necessary numbers. Between 1933 and 1964, the Zangrando and the United States Department of Commerce data were utilized.

Table 4-6

The Mean Number of Persons Lynched in the United States from 1882 to 1968

Year	White	Black	Other	Total
1882	65	48	-	133
1883	76	50	-	126
1884	155	52	-	207
1885	107	74	-	183
1886	63	74	-	137
1887	50	71	-	121
1888	69	70	-	139
1889	79	95	-	174
1890	22	88	-	110
1891	63	122	-	185
1892	79	157	-	236
1893	39	136	-	175
1894	58	132	-	190
1895	64	111	-	175
1896	48	80	-	128
1897	39	123	-	162
1898	24	102	-	126
1899	21	85	-	106
1900	10	102	-	112
1901	27	107	-	134
1902	10	86	-	96
1903	17	86	-	103
1904	7	80	-	87
1905	5	60	-	65
1906	5	64	-	69
1907	3	59	-	62
1908	8	92	-	100
1909	14	73	-	87
1910	10	73	-	83
1911	8	65	-	73
1912	4	68	-	72
1913	1	59	-	60
1914	5	55	-	60
1915	29	66	-	95
1916	6	55	-	61
1917	2	43	-	45
1918	4	62	-	66
1919	6	77	-	83
1920	8	55	-	63
1921	6	59	-	65
1922	7	52	-	59
1923	4	28	-	32
1924	0	16	-	16
1925	0	20	-	20
1926	7	25	-	32
1927	1	16	-	17
1928	1	10	-	11

Table 6 (continued)

Year	White	Black	Other	Total
1929	3	7	-	10
1930	1	20	-	21
1931	1	12	-	13
1932	2	6	-	8
1933	4	24	-	28
1934	0	15	-	15
1935	2	18	-	20
1936	0	8	-	8
1937	0	8	-	8
1938	0	6	-	6
1939	1	2	-	3
1940	1	4	-	5
1941	0	4	-	4
1942	0	6	-	6
1943	0	3	-	3
1944	0	2	-	2
1945	0	1	-	1
1946	0	6	-	6
1947	0	1	-	1
1948	1	1	-	2
1949	0	3	-	3
1950	1	1	-	2
1951	0	1	-	1
1952	0	0	-	0
1953	0	0	-	0
1954	0	0	-	0
1955	0	3	-	3
1956	0	0	-	0
1957	1	0	-	1
1958	0	0	-	0
1959	0	1	-	1
1960	0	0	-	0
1961	0	1	-	1
1962	0	0	-	0
1963	0	1	-	1
1964	2	1	-	3
Total	1356	3549	-	4905

Source: Cutler, James Elbert (1905); White, Walter (1929); Raper, Arthur F. (1933); United States Department of Commerce (Bureau of the Census); Zangrando, Robert L. (1980).

Note: There were no lynchings recorded from 1965 to 1970.

Graphical representation of the data contained in Table 4-6 is illustrated in Figure 3. The solid line in the figure represents the number of blacks lynched in the United States between 1882 and 1970, and the broken line represents the number of whites that have been lynched between 1882 and 1970. Two aspects of this graph must be kept in mind, however. First, the graph represents an "average" (statistical mean) of the number of lynchings reported by the several sources. Secondly, the numbers reported by the several data sources represent the number of "officially" known lynchings. Undoubtedly there were lynchings that were never recorded or documented and, thus, the graph probably under-represents the actual number of both black and white lynchings that took place during this period.

Figure 3

Black/White Lynchings in the United States
from 1880 to 1970.

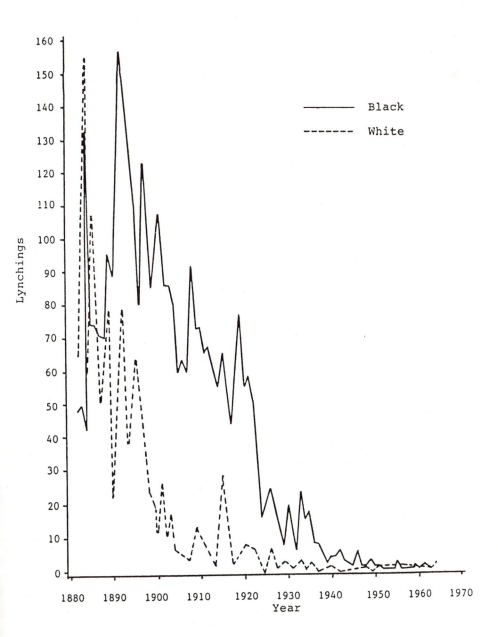

The most striking feature of the graph is the degree of disproportionality between the number of white lynchings and the number of black lynchings from 1882 to 1970. The graph shows that the largest number of whites lynched was in 1884, and that this figure accounted for 74.9% of all lynchings in that year. Cutler (1905) explains that the majority of these lynchings occurred in the Western states for murder and stealing cattle. After that year, however, the graph shows that blacks were disproportionately lynched in overwhelming numbers compared to whites. The largest number of blacks lynched was in 1892 (157). Cutler points out that during the twenty-two years he surveyed (1882-1903), the average number of blacks lynched per year was about 93, while the average for white lynchings was about 53.

The graph also shows that the number of black lynchings generally decreased after 1893 with an occasional dramatic increase or decrease, and that the number of black lynchings per year did not reach a consistent low of less than ten lynchings per year until 1936. While the number of white lynchings show the same general downward slope with sporadic peaks and valleys, the number of white lynchings reached a consistent low of less than ten per year as early as 1904. The National Association for the Advancement of Colored People (1969) reports that the increase in the number of white lynchings between 1914 and 1918 was largely due to the fact that twenty-seven Mexicans were lynched in Texas in 1915. Raper explains, however, that the general decrease in the proportion of white persons lynched is "a corollary of the fact that lynchings decreased more rapidly outside of than in the South" (1933:27). In a sense, this trend tends to indicate the extent to which lynchings had become a Southern (regional) and racial phenomenon.

Data provided by Hall (1979) tends to confirm Raper's (1933) contention. Table 4-7 shows the number of persons lynched in the United States by region and by race for five-year periods from 1889 to 1928. The table shows that between 1889 and 1893 the South accounted for 84% of the total number of lynchings in the United States, for 87.8% between 1894 and 1898, for 90.6% between 1899 and 1903, and for over 95% of the total number of lynchings for the 25-year period from 1904 to 1928.

Table 4-7

The Number of Persons Lynched in the United States from 1889 to 1928 by Race and by Region for Five Year Periods

Year	South*	Non-South	Black	White	Total
1889-1893	705	134	579	260	839
1894-1898	680	94	544	230	774
1899-1903	492	51	455	88	543
1904-1908	362	19	354	27	381
1909-1913	347	15	326	36	362
1914-1918	311	14	264	61	325
1919-1923	287	14	273	28	301
1924-1928	95	5	91	9	100
Total	3279	346	2886	739	3625

*   Alabama, Arkansas, Florida, Georgia, Kentucky, Louisiana, Mississippi, Missouri, North Carolina, Oklahoma, South Carolina, Tennessee, Texas, Virginia, West Virginia.

Source: Hall, Jacquelyn Dowd. (1979:134). Revolt Against Chivalry - Jessie Daniel Ames and the Women's Campaign Against Lynching. New York, NY: Columbia University Press.

Table 4-7 also shows that blacks have been disproportionately lynched when compared to the number of whites lynched during the same time periods. Black lynchings comprised 69% of all lynchings between 1889 and 1893, 70.2% between 1894 and 1898, and 83.8% between 1899 and 1903. Between 1904 and 1928, black lynchings accounted for well over 90% of all lynchings except for the five-year period between 1914 and 1918 when it dropped to 81%.

The data shown in Table 4-8 illustrate the extent to which lynching has been systematically relegated to the South against blacks. Table 4-8 shows that not only have Alabama, Arkansas, Florida, Georgia, Kentucky, Louisiana, Mississippi, Missouri, North Carolina, Oklahoma, South Carolina, Tennessee, Texas, Virginia, and West Virginia constituted those states with the largest number of lynchings, but they also comprise those states with the largest number of black lynchings.

Table 4-8

The Number of Persons Lynched in the United States from 1882 to 1930 by State and Race

State	White	Black	Total
Alabama*	46	296	342
Arizona	35	1	36
Arkansas*	64	230	294
California	42	4	46
Colorado	70	6	76
Connecticut	0	0	0
Delaware	0	1	1
Florida*	25	241	266
Georgia*	34	474	508
Idaho	16	6	22
Illinois	15	16	31
Indiana	33	19	52
Iowa	19	1	20
Kansas	34	18	52
Kentucky*	62	151	213
Louisiana*	60	328	388
Maine	0	0	0
Maryland	3	27	30
Massachusetts	0	0	0
Michigan	4	4	8
Minnesota	6	3	9
Mississippi*	45	500	545
Missouri*	53	63	116
Montana	91	2	93

Table 8 (continued)

State	White	Black	Total
Nebraska	55	5	60
Nevada	12	2	14
New Hampshire	0	0	0
New Jersey	0	1	1
New Mexico	39	4	43
New York	1	1	2
North Carolina*	14	85	99
North Dakota	12	2	14
Ohio	9	13	22
Oklahoma*	116	44	160
Oregon	22	3	25
Pennsylvania	1	5	6
Rhode Island	0	0	0
South Carolina*	5	154	159
South Dakota	34	0	34
Tennessee*	44	196	240
Texas*	143	349	492
Utah	6	3	9
Vermont	0	0	0
Virginia*	16	88	104
Washington	30	0	30
West Virginia*	15	35	50
Wisconsin	6	0	6
Wyoming	38	7	45
Total	1375	3386	4761

*   Southern states

Source: Hall, Jacquelyn Dowd. (1979:134-135). **Revolt Against Chivalry - Jessie Daniel Ames and the Women's Campaign Against Lynching.** New York,NY: Columbia University Press.

It can be further noted in Figure 3 that the number of black lynchings dramatically decreased sometime after about 1921. White (1929) explains this decline as due primarily to the migration of about 2 million blacks from the South to replace immigrant labor in Northern factories. As White points out, "[t]he European war shut off abruptly the flood of immigrants who for years had amply supplied the demands for unskilled labor to dig in the mines, tend the furnaces, and do the other manifold tasks of American industrial plants" (1929:110).

Other researchers have argued that this decline is due to various modernizing trends in the South. Myrdal (1944), for example, has argued that the number of black lynchings decreased as the South became less semi-isolated. Myrdal notes that rural electrification, radio, paved highways, automobiles, motion pictures, educational improvements, and even intercollegiate athletics provided southern life with meaningful alternatives to traditional beliefs and routinized behavior. Reed (1969) has also noted that journalists, business managers, and public officials (advocates of industrialism) moved to curtail evidence of violence that could tarnish the South's image to Northern investors and southern merchants and thereby retard economic growth. In addition, Zangrando (1980) points out that the mechanization of agriculture, industrial expansion, and the migration of blacks and whites from rural to urban areas within and beyond the South produced considerable change and mandated techniques of social control other than lynching. Zangrando explains that during this period blacks were systematically denied full economic participation in the South. Job opportunities that developed with the movement of northern industries to the South after the first World War were denied to blacks. As a result, blacks were unable to find relief from the economic depression of this era in the federally funded employment programs such as the CCC, TVA, and WPA because local officials were appointed to administrate the projects who advertently awarded positions almost exclusively to whites. Thus, as Zangrando argues, with blacks largely disenfranchised, segregated, and economically victimized, supremacists could dispense with lynching as an everyday means of manipulating and controlling blacks. The decline in the number of black lynchings is also viewed by Zangrando as greatly facilitated by the disclosure of brutalities associated with black lynchings by the NAACP to secure enactment of a federal anti-lynching law in 1922, 1937, and 1940.[9] (See also Grant, 1975.)

Figure 3 on black-white lynchings in the United States also shows that lynchings occurred as late as 1964. In that year three civil rights workers were lynched in Mississippi - one black and two whites. Not shown in the figure, however, is the latest documented lynching in the United States - the 1981 killing of a black teenager in Alabama. The **Associated Press** reported in February of 1987 that the family of Michael Donald had won $7 million in damages against the United Klans of America and six past and present Klansman. The press release reports further that a Klansman convicted in the killing, James Knowles, pleaded with the jury to decide in favor of the black victim's family because young Donald was abducted at random and slain to show Klan strength in Alabama and to intimidate blacks from serving on juries.

REASONS FOR LYNCHINGS (CRIMES)

According to Cutler (1905), between the years 1889 and 1903 there were 753 (38.0%) blacks lynched for murder, 675 (34.0%) lynched for rape, 206 (10.3%) lynched for minor offenses, 104 (5.2%) lynched for arson, 96 (4.8% lynched for theft crimes, 46 (2.3%) lynched for assault, 18 (.9%) lynched for desperadism (desperado), and 87 (4.3%) blacks lynched for unknown offenses. In contrast, between these same years there were 321 (53.5%) whites lynched for murder, 69 (11.5%) lynched for rape, 63 (10.5%) lynched for theft crimes, 42 (7.0%) lynched for minor offenses, 30 (5.0%) lynched for desperadism, 19 (3.2%) lynched for arson, 6 (1.0%) lynched for assault, and 50 (8.3%) lynched for crimes unknown.

The NAACP (1919, 1969) reports that between 1889 and 1918 there were 2,522 blacks and 702 whites lynched in the United States. Of the number of blacks lynched during this period, 900 (35.7%) were lynched for murder, 477 (18.9%) for rape, 237 (9.3%) for attacks upon women, 253 (10.0%) for crimes against persons, 210 (8.3%) for crimes against property, 303 (12.0%) for miscellaneous crimes, and 142 (4.6%) were lynched for no crime. For the total number of whites lynched during this period, 319 (45.0%) were lynched for murder, 46 (6.5%) for rape, 13 (1.8%) for attacks upon women, 62 (8.8%) for crimes against persons, 121 (17.2%) for crimes against property, 135 (18.8%) for miscellaneous crimes, and 6 (.8%) were lynched for no crime.

Raper (1933) contends that the data secured from **The Negro Year Book, 1931-1932** shows that between 1889 and 1932 there were 1,406 (37.6%) blacks lynched for murder, 215 (5.7%) for felonious assault, 878 (23.5%) for rape and attempted rape, 267 (7.1%) for robbery and thelft, 67 (1.7%) for insults to whites, and 902 (24.1%) blacks were lynched for "all other causes." Using statistics provided by the Tuskegee Institute, Zangrando (1980) has shown that out of the 4,743 blacks lynched between 1882 and 1968, 1,937 (40.8%) were lynched for murder, 1,200 (25.3%) for rape and attempted rape, 1,084 (22.9%) for "all other causes," 232 (4.9%) for robbery and theft, 205 (4.3%) for felonious assault, and 85 (1.8%) for insulting a white person.

The preceding review of data sources also show that blacks comprise the **racial** category of persons most often lynched for murder, rape, and absurdly trivial crimes. The data show that while both blacks and whites were most often lynched for murder, blacks were lynched for rape as often as they were lynched for murder. Where whites were often lynched for theft crimes, blacks were more often lynched for minor offenses bordering on "senselessness." The absurdity of crime for which blacks were often lynched is further illustrated by White (1929) who notes that in 1918 a mother and her two young daughters were killed by a mob in Texas when they "threatened a white man."

Cutler (1905) explains that the crime of murder included actual murder, accessory to murder, suspected murder, alleged murder, conspiracy to murder, and complicity in murder. Rape included actual rape, attempted rape, and alleged rape. It is the difference in minor offenses between blacks and whites, however, that illustrates the extent to which blacks were lynched for almost any frivolous reason. Cutler lists the minor offenses for which blacks and whites were lynched. Minor offenses for whites included:

> "wife beating, cruelty, kidnapping, saloon keeping, turning state's evidence, refusing to turn statte's evidence, being obnoxious, swindling, political prejudice, seduction, giving information, frauds, informing, protection of a black, giving evidence, mob indignation, illicit distilling, disorderly conduct, incest, elopement, revenue informer, disreputable character, arrest of a miner, aiding escape of murderer, suspected of killing cattle, and prospective elopement" (1905:167).

For blacks, however, minor offenses included crimes bordering even more on the ridiculous:

> "grave robbery, threatened political exposures, slander, self-defense, wife beating, cutting levees, kidnapping, voodooism, poisoning horses, writing insulting letters, incendiary language, swindling, jilting a girl, colonizing negroes, turning state's evidence, throwing stones, unpopularity, making threats, circulating scandals, being troublesome, bad reputation, drunkenness, strike rioting, insults, supposed offense, insulting women, fraud, criminal abortion, alleged stock poisoning, enticing servant away, writing letter to white

women, asking white woman in marriage, conspiracy, introducing smallpox, giving information, conjuring, to prevent evidence, being disreputable, informing, concealing a criminal, slapping a child, shooting at police, passing counterfeit money, felony, elopement with a white girl, refusing to give evidence, giving evidence, disobeying ferry regulations, running guarantine, violation of contract, paying attention to white girl, resisting assault, inflammatory language, resisting arrest, testifying for one of his own race, keeping gambling-house, quarrel over profit sharing, forcing white boy to commit crime, and lawlessness" (1905:167).

Comparison of these two lists reveals that some of the offenses for which blacks were lynched were specifically designed to restrict inter-racial contact between black men and white women. For example, lynching offenses for blacks included such crimes as "insulting women," "writing a letter to a white woman," and "elopement with a white girl." Conversely, there were no such lynching offenses directed toward defining the degree of social tolerance of relations between black women and white men. The lack of any such offense meant that interracial sex between black women and white men was a prerogative that "white males meant to enjoy." Zangrando (1980) points out that black women were consequently "open to sexual attack" by white men. The pervasiveness of this form of social contact is further illustrated by the fact that "no white has ever been executed (legally or illegally) for the rape of a black" (Marable, 1984:121).

The alleged propensity for sex crimes against white women by black men was unprecedented in the South before 1830. White (1929) notes that for the two centuries before 1830, beginning in 1619 when black slaves were first brought to America, charges of rape against a black man were unknown. Given the population of black slaves during that period, there was considerable opportunity for such crimes. Moreover, "[c]harges of rape were made with increasing frequency as a greater number of lynchings and more brutal methods of execution of the victims brought vehement condemnation of lynching from other parts of the society" (White, 1929:89). The rpae myth, therefore, amounted to nothing more than a hedonistic rationale for the white lynch mob to justify its control over blacks (e.g., the protection of white women).

BESTIALITY OF LYNCHING

The most inhuman conduct ever imaginable has characterized black lynchings in the United States. White (1929) has remarked that lynchings often entailed a beastiality unknown even to the most remote and uncivilized parts of the world. The horrors that have been suffered by blacks at the hands of white lynch mobs compare to the atrocities suffered by more than 12 million persons in the Nazi death camps. Men, women, and children have been burned to death, had their bodies burned after death, and beaten and dismembered to death. Marable (1984:15) explains, for example, that some of the slaves who had participated in the Nat Turner rebellion of 1831 "were beheaded and their skulls were positioned on polls on the public roads," and that the dried skin of Turner himself had been sewn into souvenir purses. White (1929) points out that of the 416 blacks that American mobs lynched between 1918 and 1927, forty-two of the victims were burned alive, sixteen were burned after death, and eight of the victims were beaten to death or cut to pieces. Marable (1984:119) adds that some were simply tied to the backs of automobiles and dragged across city streets until they were unconscious: "Many Black men were tied down and brutally castrated with knives or axes." Raper reports that in Georgia in 1930, a black man by the name of James Irwin "was jabbed in the mouth with a sharp pole...his toes were cut off joint by joint...his fingers were similarly removed...his teeth were extracted with wire pliers...(his) body was saturated with gasoline and a lighted match was applied...and hundreds of shots were fired into the dying victim" (1933:6-7). Snead (1986) explains that Claude Neal, a young black lynched for murder in 1934 in Florida was subjected to ten hours of grievous torture involving castration and self-cannibalism. More graphically, McGovern writes that "Claude Neal's penis and testicles were cut off and that he was forced to eat them" (1982:80).

Two actual accounts of earlier lynchings will further suffice the point here. The first story was published, in part, in the **New York Tribune** and the Vicksburg, Mississippi, **Evening Post** on February 8, 1904. The **Tribune** reported that Luther Holbert and his wife had been burned at the stake for the murder of a white planter named James Eastland. The newspapers wrote that two innocent blacks were shot by the posse looking for Holberty, and that his wife could in no way be implicated in the murder of Eastland. The **Evening Post** reported the following story:

> "When the two Negroes were captured, they were tied to trees and while the funeral pyres were being prepared they were forced to suffer the most fiendish tortures. The blacks were forced to hold out their hands while one finger at a time was chopped off. The fingers were distributed as souvenirs. The ears of the murderers were cut off. Holbert was beaten severely, his skull was fractured, and one of his eyes, knocked out with a stick, hung by a shred from the socket... The most excruciating form of punishment consisted in the use of large corkscrew in the hands of some of the mob. This instrument was bored into the flesh of the man and woman, in the arms, legs and body, and they pulled out, the spirals tearing out big pieces of raw, quivering flesh every time it was withdrawn" (White, 1929:35-36).

The second account was first published in **The Lynchings of May, 1918, in Brooks and Lowndes Counties, Georgia:**

> "An unscrupulous farmer in south Georgia refused to pay a Negro hand wages due him. A few days later the farmer was shot and killed. Not finding the Negro suspected of the murder, mobs began to kill every Negro who could even remotely be connected with the victim and the alleged slayer. One of these was a man named Hayes Turner, whose offense was that he knew the alleged slayer.... To Turner's wife, within one month of accouchement, was brought the news of her husband's death.... Word of her threat to swear out warrants for the arrest of her husband's murderers came to them. 'We'll teach the damn' nigger wench some sense,' was their answer, as they began to seek her. Sunday morning, with a hot May sun beating down, they found her. Securely they bound her ankles together and, by them, hanged her to a tree. Gasoline and motor oil were thrown upon her dangling clothes; a match wrapped her in sudden flames.... 'Mister, you ought to've heard the nigger wench howl!' a member of the mob boasted to me a few days later as we stood at the place of Mary Turner's death.... The clothes burned from her crispy toasted body, in which, unfortunately, life still lingered, a man stepped towards the woman and, with his knife, ripped open the abdomen in a crude Caesarean operation. Out tumbled the prematurely born child. Two feeble cries it gave - and received for answer the heel of a stalwart man, as life was ground out of the tiny form. Under the tree of death was scooped a shallow hole. The rope about Mary Turner's charred ankles was cut, and swiftly her body tumbled into its grave. Not without a sense of humour or of appropriateness was some member of the mob. An empty whisky-bottle, quart size, was given for headstone. Into its neck was stuck a half- smoked cigar - which

had saved the delicate nostrils of one member of the mob from the stench of burning human flesh" (White, 1929:27-29).

PUBLIC SENTIMENT TOWARD THE LYNCHING OF BLACKS

The extent to which the lynching of blacks was sanctioned by the general public is not only illustrated by the hideous barbarism that characterized these lynchings, but also be the fact that lynchings were almost always accompanied by jubilant public fanfare. Raper (1933) has pointed out that the lynch mobs of the 1930's totaled some 75,000 men, women, and children. The presence of women in the crowd acted to "inspire the mob to greater brutalities." Literally thousands of people are said to have ridden out from miles around to see the site where James Irwin was lynched in Ocilla, Georgia, in 1930. McGovern (1982) reports that between three- and four-hundred people participated in the lynching of Claude Neal in 1934. Marable (1984) explains that the thrill seekers were often after body parts that could be claimed as souvenirs.

Chadbourn (1933) analyzed newspaper reports of convictions of lynchers gathered by the Tuskegee Institute. Chadbourn found that only about eight-tenths of one percent of the lynchings in the United States since 1900 ended in conviction of the lynchers. He reports that Alabama (4%), Georgia (.8%), Oklahoma (3%), Virginia (4%), Minnesota (3%), and Texas (.7%) are those states that have had any significant percentages of convictions. That is, over 99% of all persons who have actively participated in lynchings have escaped arrest, prosecution, conviction, and punishment.

The silent acquiescence of court officials and law enforcement officers illustrates the extent to which public sentiment supported lynching, and it is also a major reason why the courts were ineffective in punishing lynchers. Zangrando (1980) notes that the silence and inaction of public officials was primarily due to the fact that they were answerable to a white constituency. For this reason, coroner's juries often found that lynched blacks had died "at the hands of parties unknown." Raper (1933) has listed several factors that made courts ineffective: divided responsibility between peace officers, judges, and grand and trial juries; the indifference of court officials; the widespread feeling that white women should be shielded from court testimony; the disinclination of local jurymen to indict or convict their neighbors; and promises made the mob by officers and leading citizens in order to prevent further outbreaks.

Pro-lynching sentiment of public officials is also illustrated by the fact that police officers often aided in black lynchings or were simply indifferent to them. Sheriffs were usually part of the townspeople who harbored the same vehement passions against blacks as the majority of citizenry. For example, during the course of one lynching police officers are reported by Raper to have "directed traffic while the corpse was dragged through the streets" (1933:13). He also explains that "...[i]n most cases the sheriff and his deputies merely stood by while the mob did its work, and later reported that the mob had taken them by surprise, or that, though aware of the impending danger, they were unwilling to shoot into the crowd lest they kill innocent men, women, and children" (Raper, 1933:13).

CONTRASTING LEGAL EXECUTIONS WITH ILLEGAL EXECUTIONS

Although it can be argued that illegal executions are not comparable with legal executions because illegal executions are imposed without legal authority, there are other aspects of these two forms of execution that are justifiably comparable. Bowers (1974) explains that both forms of execution share striking similarities. Both forms of execution represent the action of the community to punish transgressors of basic social mores: (a) both are forms of retributive justice and designed to deter others from perpetrating like crimes; (b) both are performed by representatives of the entire community; (c) both employ similar methods of imposing death (shooting and hanging); and (d) both have attracted public exhibition and fanfare. In addition, while illegal executions are imposed beyond the authority of the state, the indifference of public officials, law enforcement officers, and court officials toward lynching tends to proffer and aire of sanction which effectively communicates the idea that illegal executions were not imposed without legal authority.

Figure 4 contrasts the total number of illegal executions (lynchings) with the total number of legal executions of prisoners under civil authority in the United States between 1850 and 1970. The data on lynchings are contained in Table 4-7 and, as noted, are a compilation of the computed means from various data sources reporting different numbers of lynchings for each year between 1882 and 1970. The data on legal executions have been taken from the Teeters and Zibulka (1974) inventory of 5,708 executions conducted under state authority in the United States from 1853 to 1967.[10]

Figure 4

Legal and Illegal Executions in the United States
from 1850 to 1970

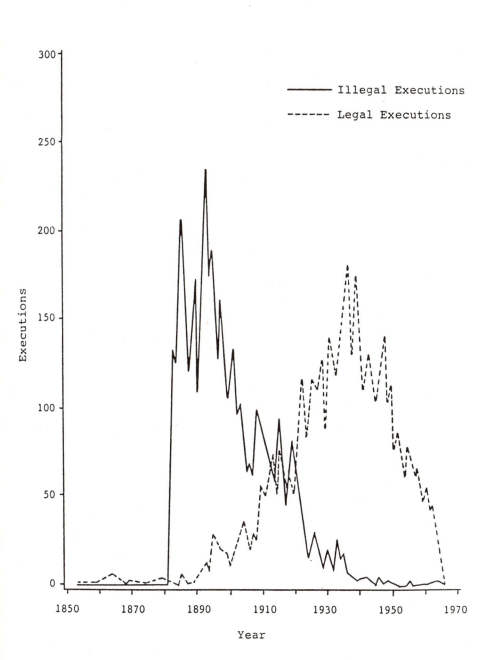

There are several interesting aspects about the relationship between illegal and legal executions that are revealed in Figure 4. The most dramatic feature of the graph is that it clearly illustrates that the power to execute social undesirables has simply shifted from the hands of the lynch mob to the power of the state. Although the graph shows that the power to execute has never fully resided in either the lynch mob or the state, evidenced by the fact that both illegal and legal executions have taken place throughout the entire time span of the graph, the graph shows that dominant power to execute shifted from the lynch mob to the state as late as 1921. That is, the number of legal executions did not exceed the number of illegal executions in the United States until 1921. As noted, the demise of illegal executions in the South after 1921 was the result of modernizing trends, migration of blacks beyond the South, and disclosure of the atrocities that usually characterized the lynching of blacks. Bowers has argued that "the increasing number of state imposed executions from 1890 to 1930 should be understood not so much as 'growth' but as a 'transfer' of executions from one locus of authority to another" (1974:44).

At first glance, the graph appears to show that more people have been executed illegally than legally. The data show, however, that of the 10,613 persons executed between 1850 and 1970 there were 4,905 (46.2%) persons illegally executed and 5,708 (53.7%) persons legally executed - a difference of 803 executions. It must be kept in mind, however, that there is no available data on the number of lynchings that occurred between 1853, when the first state-imposed execution took place in the District of Columbia, and 1882 when the first "officially" recorded lynchings took place. Table 4-9 tends to show, then, that if one were to consider the number of lynchings that undoubtedly took place between 1853 and 1882, and the number of executions performed under "local" authority before the 1890's, the overall proportion of lynchings to legal executions may significantly increase.[11] The table shows that there were about 1,060 local executions and about 1,593 illegal executions during the 1890's. Although Bowers (1974) argues that the movement from local- authority to state- authorized executions was not readily adopted by the several states until the 1890's, the problem becomes discerning the historical circumstances under which illegal executions become defined as legal executions before the 1890's.

Table 4-9

The Number of Persons Executed in the United States by Decade from the 1890's to the 1980's

Years	State Authority*	Local Authority**	Illegal Executions***	Total
1890's	154	1,060	1,593	2,807
1900's	275	901	915	2,091
1910's	625	406	698	1,729
1920's	1,030	131	325	1,487
1930's	1,520	147	130	1,797
1940's	1,174	110	33	1,317
1950's	682	35	8	725
1960's	191	0	5	196
1970's	3****	0	0	3
1980's	58	0	1	59
Totals	5,712	2,790	3,708	12,212

*   Source: Teeters, N.K. and C.J. Zibulka. (1974). "Executions Under State Authority." In William J. Bowers' **Executions in America**. Lexington, MA: D.C. Heath and Company.

**   Source: Bowers, Willaim J. (1974). **Executions in America**. Lexington, MA: D.C. Heath and Company.

***   Source: The mean number of lynchings calculated from Cutler (1905), White (1969), Raper (1933), the United States Department of Commerce (Bureau of the Census - 1975), and Zangrando (1980).

****   Source: United States Department of Justice (Bureau of Justice Statistics). (1985). **Sourcebook**. Washington D.C.: United States Government Printing Office.

Reichel, Philip L. and Lisa Munden. (May, 1987). "Media Coverage of Executions." Unpublished manuscript. University of Northern Colorado. Presented at the 58th annual meeting of the Pacific Sociological Association in Eugene, Oregon.

The graph also shows that increases in the number of illegal and legal executions corresponds almost simultaneously with increases in the other form of exectuion. That is, every peak in the line representing illegal executions corresponds to a peak in the line representing legal executions, and conversely. This phenomenon suggests that both illegal and legal executions are subject to the same social forces giving rise to executions in general.

While not directly contrasted in the graph, another point of contention between legal and illegal executions is disproportionate and discriminatory application of the death penalty to blacks. The data on lynchings, shown in Table 4-6, reveal that 72.3% of the 4,905 illegal executions performed between 1882 and 1970 were blacks, and 27.6% were white executions. The Teeters-Zibulka data show that of the 5,708 state-authorized exectuions between 1854 and 1967, 45.8% were whtie and 52.2% were black executions. Also, the United States Bureau of Justice Statistics (1985) reports that between 1930 and 1984 there were 3,891 prisoners executed under civil authority in the United States. Of these figures, 2,067 (53.1%) were black and 1,773 (45.5%) were white.

Racial disparity in imposing the death penalty becomes even more clearly defined among executions for rape. As noted, Cutler (1905), Raper (1933), the NAACP (1969), and Zangrando (1980) have shown that the crime of rape, attempted rape, or alleged rape constitutes a major percentage of the classified causes for the lynching of blacks. Similarly, official criminal justice statistics on the number of prisoners legally executed between 1930 and 1982 reveal that 405 (89%) blacks and 48 (11%) whites were executed for the crime of rape. The South executed 98.3% of all blacks executed for rape. While the north central region of the country executed the remaining seven blacks for rape, the western and northwestern sections have never executed a black for rape. The District of Columbia, Virginia, West Virginia, Mississippi, Louisiana and Oklahoma have never executed a white for the crime rape. The Teeters-Zibulka data show that between 1853 and 1964 the number of blacks executed for rape constituted 88.8% of all persons executed for rape, and that whites comprised 10.3% of the total.

Given that blacks have consistently represented about 12% of the total American population, these statistics overwhelmingly indicate that the death penalty has been disproportionately applied to blacks. Blacks have been executed for murder at over five times the rate of executions for whties, and blacks have been executed for rape at about nine times the execution rate than whites. Thesse statistics alone do not show that racial discrimination has characterized the imposition of the death penalty to blacks. But a number of empirically-based studies have shown that in the case of blacks, disproportionality in the application of the death penalty amounts to racial discrimination. That is, empirical studies have established rather pervasive evidence that the death penalty has not only been disproportionately applied to blacks convicted of rape and murder, but that the death penalty has been imposed on black prisoners in a discretionary and discriminatory manner.

Many studies have documented evidence of racial discrimination in the imposition of the death penalty on blacks. A review of these studies in relation to whether they were conducted before,[12] during the interim, or after the United States Supreme Court decisions in **Furman v. Georgia**[13] (1972) and **Gregg v. Georgia**[14] (1976) reveals two substantive conclusions. First, despite the attempts by the Court in **Furman** and **Gregg** to thwart racial discrimination in the use of the capital punishment, the death penalty continues to be imposed against blacks in a capricious manner. Second, the specific finding by many of the studies that blacks who victimize whites consistently have the highest probability of receiving a capital sentence tends to substantiate the claim that capital punishment serves the extralegal function of majority group protection; namely, the daeth penalty acts to safeguard (through deterrence) that class of individuals (whites) who are least likely to be victimized.

The death penalty continues to be imposed to blacks in a capricious manner. That is, the evidence tends to confirm the hypothesis that arbitrariness is an inherent characteristic of the use of the death penalty. Studies by Riedel (1976) and Arkin (1980) show that the same degree of racial disparity present in pre-**Furman** cases is also prevalent in post-**Furman** cases. That is, the **Furman** decision had little or no diminishing effect on the extent to which black capital offenders were subjected to racial discrimination in imposition of the death penalty. Studies by Boris (1979), Swigert and Farrel (1976), Gross and Mauro (1984), Bowers (1983), and Gross (1985) all show that the death penalty was still used as a mechanism by which to protect a specific class of individuals - namely whites - from criminal victimization. Black defendants whose victims were white were overwhelmingly convicted and sentenced to death when compared to other racial categories of defendant-victim. Several other studies have also shown that the safeguards for guided discretion in the use of the death penalty have failed to correct for the racial disparities. Specific analyses have shown that as long as individual prosecutors continue to have broad-based discretion to select which cases they will try as capital cases, racial discrimination in application of the death penalty will undoubtedly continue.[15] Racial discrimination in the use of the death penalty has also been found to be perpetuated through the appellate review of capital cases. (See Radelet and Vandiver, 1983.) The irony here is that the appellate courts were highly touted in **Gregg** as the foremost safeguard against unguided discretion in the application of the death penalty.

Various studies have shown that black defendants with white victims have been overwhelmingly convicted and sentenced to death when compared to other defendant-victim racial categories. Wolfgang (1974), for example, found that race was the only statistically significant variable that could account for the disproportionate application of the death penalty to blacks convicted of rape. Other empirical studies show that blacks convicted of raping a white woman comprise the most execution-prone offender group. Gross and Mauro (1984) have provided rather persuasive evidence that blacks who kill whites are much more likely to be sentenced to death than any other racial combination of defendant-victim. These findings clearly show that when whites are the victims of heinous crimes perpetrated by blacks, punishment is more harsh. Racism has become so well entrenched and routinized in the imposition of the death penalty that it has developed into a systematic pattern of differential treatment of blacks that is specifically designed to protect members of the dominant white group. While a preponderance of contemporary authors and jurists writing on theories of crime and punishment readily cite retribution and deterrence as foremost rationales for imposing the death penalty on those who commit heinous crimes, empirical studies show that the death penalty serves the extralegal function of protecting whites.

Empirically-based evidence that racial discrimination continues to influence the imposition of the death penalty has literally been ignored by the court in **McClesky v. Kemp**[16] (1987). The proposed safeguards that surround application of the death penalty amount to no safeguards at all. The only substantive conclusion that can be drawn from review of **Furman, Gregg,** and **McClesky** is that the court has moved from a postition of formally recognizing that imposition of the death penalty is imbued with racial prejudice (**Furman**), to a position of sanctioning racial prejudice as a cost of imposing the penalty (**McClesky**). It appears from the cases handed down from the court that racism is a legitimate penological doctrine. For the advocates of racial and ethnic equality, the death penalty cannot be morally justified on the premise that racial oppression, subjugation, and social subservience are legitimate liabilities of maintaining social order. Social order under these circumstances amounts to social order predicated upon racism.

CONCLUDING REMARKS

The most substantive observation that can be made from this analysis of lynchings in the United States is that lynchings have been utilized as a repressive mechanism for the systematic maintenance of black persons in subservient social positions and subjugated social rules relative to white persons. Data has been presented which shows that blacks were not only disproportionately lynched when compared to whites, but that black lynchings have entailed the most insidious forms of barbarism and torture. It has been suggested that the rationale for the lynching of blacks was rooted in the fear whites had for the economic, social, and political progress that blacks began to experience during Reconstruction. As a result, the rape myth was specifically inviting to the white lynch mob because it gave a credence to black lynchings that otherwise was impossible to justify. Finally, the most disheartening fact about the history of legal and illegal execution of blacks in the United States is that the power to execute has simply transferred from the hands of the lynch mob to the power of the state.

CHAPTER FIVE

AN EMPIRICAL ANALYSIS OF SOCIO-CULTURAL KNOWLEDGE: RACIAL PREJUDICE AND THE DEATH PENALTY

Social scientific analysis of the relationship between racial prejudice and public support for the death penalty is important because its findings have potential legal significance. In **Furman v. Georgia** (1972), for example, all nine justices of the United States Supreme Court relied, in part, on attitudinal survey data concerning capital punishment to determine the unconstitutionality of the death penalty. Specifically, Justice Marshall argued that capital punishment is without constitutional validity when the penalty is reprehensible to "currently existing moral values." Gelles and Straus have pointed out that it is unlikely for Supreme Court Justices to discount public sentiment on the death penalty "unless it can be shown that the public view is based on standards or reflects conditions which the Court would be reluctant to accept or encourage" (1975:611). Where it can be shown, then, that public sentiment toward the death penalty is imbued with racial prejudice, it would certainly mean that public opinion on capital punishment reflects socio-cultural values that are inconsistent with a society that espouses an egalitarian standard of social justice.

Our purpose in this chapter is to examine the extent to which racial prejudice influences public opinion on the death penalty. The main research question addressed in this chapter is - "How does white racial prejudice against black persons influence white public opinion concerning the death penalty?" The following research questions are also addressed in this chapter: Are older persons more likely to favor the death penalty than younger persons because older persons are more racially prejudiced than younger persons? When compared with women, are men more likely to be racially prejudiced and to favor the death penalty? Are educated persons less likely to favor the death penalty because they are less likely to be racially prejudiced than persons who are not educated? Are persons who reside in the southern regions of the country more likely to harbor punitive racist attitudes than persons who reside in non-southern regions of the nation? Finally, since public opinion polls focusing on public sentiment toward capital punishment have also revealed that people who fear criminal victimization favor the death penalty more than people who do not fear criminal victimization, we will examine the relationship between fear of criminal victimization and public support for the death penalty.

RACIAL BELIEFS AND VALUES

People's racist values and beliefs tend to surface and become dominant factors in their attitudes and opinions when they are directly challenged by a major social event focused on black-white relations. For example, analyses of white public sentiments toward busing for racial balance (Sears, et al., 1972; McConashay, 1982), affirmative action programs (Jacobson, 1985), and voting behavior (Kinder and Sears, 1981) reveal that white persons respond to social problems involving black-white relations in terms of racial prejudice. In keeping with these findings, Taylor, et al. (1979) and Stinchcombe, et al. (1980) have shown that opposition to busing for racial balance is strongly related to support for the death penalty. These researchers explain that the busing issue has become linked in the public mind to an emerging ideology about crime and the appropriate treatment of criminals. In addition, the finding that busing for racial balance is related to support for the death penalty means that white public attitudes toward the death penalty must be defined in terms of social-political values based on racial prejudice. It follows then that whites may view the problem of crime as a threat against their social well-being, and that imposition of the death penalty is seen as a pragmatic solution to the growing problem of crime.[17]

The findings by Taylor, et al. (1979) and Stinchcombe, et al. (1980) are supported by a series of other studies proposing that a person's perception of increasing crime rates is directly associated with their fear of victimization and a willingness to emply punishment as a response to criminality. (See Thomas and Miller, 1980; Thomas and Foster, 1975; Thomas and Howard, 1977; Thomas and Cage, 1976; Vidmar, 1974; Vidmar and Ellsworth, 1974; Sarat and Vidmar, 1976; Rankin, 1979; Fattah, 1979.) According to these studies, one's fear of victimization is also related to a willingness to support a punitive reaction to crime and to the belief that punishment deters crime. Furthermore, these studies show that a strong correlation exists between support for capital punishment and those people who are willing to employ punishment. As Thomas and Foster have concluded, increases in the level of public support for the death penalty "can be interpreted as an understandable consequence of the widely held belief that crime rates are going up rapidly; the average citizen is in danger of becoming the victim of a criminal offense; and the deeply ingrained belief that punishment provides an effective means by which we can control deviant and criminal behavior" (1975:654).

PUBLIC OPINION

Public opinion polls focusing on the death penalty show ever increasing support for capital punishment since 1966. Gallup (1985) has found public attitudes favoring the death penalty for persons convicted of murder increasing from 51% in 1969 to 72% in 1985. These figures are consistent with National Opinion Research Center (NORC) findings of an increase in public support for capital punishment from 52% in 1972 to 70% in 1984 (Davis, 1980; Davis and Smith, 1984). Since people support harsher punitive sanctions (i.e., capital punishment) during periods of an increased social salience of the crime problem, it would appear from these findings that there has been an increase in public concern over the growing problem of crime in recent years.[18]

A 1981 Gallup report, in fact, reveals that crime is perceived as the uppermost problem facing many American neighborhoods. Fifty-four percent of those persons surveyed believed that there was more crime in their neighborhoods than a year ago. This figure represents a marked increase from 43% in 1977. Seventy-five percent of the respondents expressed the belief that criminals are becoming more violent than five years earlier. The report shows that people avoid going out alone at night, stay away from dangerous areas even during the daytime, and that people carry all types of weapons for their protection. The report further shows that 25% of the households surveyed had been victimized at least once in a twelve month period with either property stolen or a member of the household physically accosted. Some 92% of the respondents surveyed have taken preventative measures to lessen their vulnerability to crime - from 84% who make sure their doors are locked at night to 16% who have purchased firearms for protection.

In terms of capital punishment, a more recent Gallup (1985) poll shows that 71% of the white respondents hold that even if they were provided with new evidence that showed the death penalty does not act as a deterrent to murder they would still favor the death penalty. (See also Ellsworth and Ross, 1983). Sixty-four percent of these respondents who believe that the death penalty is a deterrent to the commitment of murder believe that the penalty lowers the crime rate. Some 58% of the white respondents surveyed also believe that the death penalty is a more appropriate penalty for murder than life imprisonment with no possibility for parole.

Only 31% of the white respondents surveyed thought that life imprisonment should be the ultimate penalty for murder.

RACIAL EQUALITY

Despite the lack of empirical research on the influence of racism on public opinion about the death penalty, a considerable amount of evidence has been gathered which shows a general trend of increased support for the equal treatment of blacks in American society since the early 1940's. In June of 1942, the NORC found that 42% of the white respondents surveyed answered "yes" to whether they thought "[n]egroes are as intelligent as white people; that is, can they learn just as well if they are given the same education and training" (Simon, 1974:57). Subsequent surveys conducted by the NORC have shown that the percentage of respondents favoring this belief increased to about 44% in 1944, to 53% in 1946, to 77% in 1956, and losing a percentage point to 76% in 1963.

Harris and Associates have found this trend toward egalitarianism continuing through the 1960's and 1970's. Respondents were asked whether they agreed with the statement that "blacks have less native intelligence than whites" (William et al., 1979). The percentage of respondents who disagreed with this statement rose from 61% in 1963 to 73% in 1978. The percentage of respondents who disagreed with the statement that "blacks are inferior to white people" also increased form 61% in 1963 to 85% in 1978. Although Simon (1974) points out that these findings tend to show that Americans are becoming noticeably more acceptable of the "inherent-equality' doctrine, William, et al. (1978) explain that analyses of black responses from the Harris surveys show that blacks still believe that discrimination remains a dominant aspect of their lives, and that feelings of alienation are increaing among blacks.

A series of studies conducted on NORC data from 1942 to 1985 have consistently found that white Americans have become increasingly more favorable of equal treatment for black persons (Hyman and Sheatsley, 1956, 1964; Sheatsley, 1966; Greeley and Sheatsley, 1971; Taylor, Sheatsley and Greeley, 1978; Case and Greeley, 1985a). For example, although these studies reveal that younger, more educated, and non-southern whites are particularly more accepting of racial integration, this trend is nonetheless prevalent across all age groups, levels of educational attainment, and all regions of the country. Yet, these studies also show that there are substantial numbers of white persons who hold negative attitudes toward blacks. Condran specifically warns that white Americans simply may have "improved their confirmity to the increasingly institutionalized normative standard of an officially 'liberal' society" (1979:474).

SOCIAL DESCRIPTORS

Of those studies that have empirically investigated public opinion data on captial punishment - gender, age, race, region, and the level of educational attainment - are sociodemographic variables often found as attitudinal correlates of the death penalty. People favoring the death penalty tend to be older, less educated, male, white, and from the South. For example, Smith (1976) has analyzed NORC data over a number of years and reports that the average attitudinal difference between males and females on the issue of capital punishment to be about 11.5 percentage points, but that this difference decreased to 7.5% in 1975. Erskine's (1970) assessment of numerous polls conducted in the United States shows that the difference between men and women's attitudes toward capital punishment surveyed by Gallup consistently indicates a greater number of men supporting the death penalty than women throughout the early 1960's. Harris surveys conducted during the early 1970's reveal that the attitudinal differences between males and females about the death penalty has decreased from 15% in 1970 to 10% in 1973. Snortum and Asher (1972) note that women are generally more lenient in their punitive attitudes than men. From these findings it would then appear that an increase in the social salience of the crime problem has more of an effect on the punitive attitudes of men than it has on the punitive attitudes of women.

Age is also a relevant factor in accounting for variance in public support for the death penalty. It appears that younger cohorts are far less likely to favor the death penalty than older cohorts. The findings suggest that younger people have been less fervently socialized to a punitive ideology than older people and, therefore, during periods of an increase in the social salience of crime are less likely to favor the death penalty than older cohorts. Stinchcombe, et al. (1980), for example, report fairly steady relationships between age and punitiveness over time, and argue that those persons born between 1940 and 1955 (the youngest group studied) were 10% more lenient than older cohorts. The latest data from Gallup (1985) also show the youngest cohorts of respondents (18-24 years of age) expressing the least amount of support for the death penalty (69%). The 1973 Harris survey also identifies the youngest cohort (18-29 years of age) as favoring the death penalty least (52%) when compared to those people between the ages of 30-49 (59%) and over 50 years of age (64%). Alston (1976) has found that Americans who are younger hold less punitive attitudes than those who are older. Abney and Moore (1978) have substantiated these and other such findings and argue that youth is a demonstrable social indicator of less punitive attitudes.

The polls also show that people with higher levels of education are less supportive of the death penalty than are people with lower levels of education. The 1970 Harris poll indicates that 42% of the respondents with a high school education favored the death penalty while only 36% of the respondents with a college education favored the death penalty. In 1973, Harris shows that these percentages increased to 63% for high school graduates, and to 53% for college graduates. NORC data on educational differences in levels of support for the death penalty are consistent with the Harris surveys. For the ten year period between 1972 and 1982, the NORC reported generally higher levels of support for capital punishment for people with grade school and high school educations than people with college educations (McGarrel and Flanagan, 1984:242-243). The 1972, 1976, and 1985 Gallup polls reveal, however, that higher educational levels are not indicative of less support for the death penalty, and that increases are not as dramatic as reported by Harris and NORC. The 1972 Gallup poll shows that 67% of those with high school levels of education, and 59% of the college educated favor the death penalty. In 1976, these percentages did not increase for grade school respondents (62%) or college graduates (52%), but did increase for high school graduates (69%). The 1985 Gallup poll shows that respondents with some college (76%) favor the death penalty more than those respondents with less than high school levels of education (65%).

There are a number empirical studies which show that formal education reduces white racial prejudice toward blacks. As early as 1955, Samuel Stouffer suggested that individuals who were more educated supported liberal values more than people who were less educated. A series of **Scientific American** reports on racial attitudes have, in fact, found education to be a statistically significant social factor in reducing white prejudicial attitudes toward minorities. (See Hyman and Sheatsley, 1956, 1964; Greeley and Sheatsley, 1971; Taylor, Sheatsley and Greeley, 1978; Case and Greeley, 1985a; Campbell, 1971; Condran, 1979; and Smith, 1981.)

In particular, in their analysis of the nature of education's effect on egalitarian attitudes toward blacks, Case and Greeley (1985b) contend that education increases support for racial equality because the more educated acquire greater access to sources of accurate information about a wide variety of aspects of their cultural environment. That is, education increases cultural knowledge, which, in turn broadens the individual's perspective beyond that of the local community, family or regional group. Access to more accurate information concerning the cultural environment is basically gained through increased literacy. The more educated individuals learn that racial differences are not the result of different origins and potentials, but rather stem from differences in appropriate "role models, rewards, expectations, opportunities, and advantages." Individuals with higher levels of educational experience have more contact with diverse cultural groups. "(B)oth greater education and greater cultural knowledge provide greater contact with the potential for more understanding of cultural elements, meanings, and relationships beyond those of the local community and kinship group.... Thus, the effect of having more cultural knowledge and more years of participation within the educational institution are forces tending to contradict supremacist ideologies" (Case and Greeley, 1985b:4-6). From this perspective, then, people with higher levels of educational attainment are less racist and, therefore, people with more education should be less likely to exhibit racist punitive attitudes during an increase in the environmental salience of the crime problem than people with lower levels of educational attainment. Coherent ideologies developed by the more educated on the problem of crime may not be imbued with racial prejudice because the more educated have more accurate information on possible causes of crime which do not involve racial issues.

Public opinion polls focusing on capital punishment issues reveal somewhat conflicting findings on regional differences in public support for the death penalty. A 1974 Gallup poll has found that 66% of the people residing in the South supported the death penalty for persons convicted of murder, while 63% of the respondents living in the west, midwest, and east favored the death penalty. In 1976, Gallup reported, however, that southern respondents supported capital punishment less than non-southern respondents. The results of this particular survey showed that 59% of the southern respondents supported capital punishment, while 65% of the respondents surveyed in the east, and 70% of the respondents questioned in the west and midwest favored the death penalty. In 1985, however, 74% of the southern respondents favored the death penalty and 71% of the western, midwestern, and eastern respondents supported the punishment for persons convicted of murder. In contrast to the Gallup polls, the NORC reports that between 1972 and 1980 people from the southern regions of the country favored the death penalty less than people residing in other parts of the country. In 1972, 41% of the southern respondents favored the death penalty. This percentage increased to 66% in 1980. The average percentage of the non-southern respondents favoring the death penalty rose from 59% in 1977, to 69% in 1977, and fell to 68% in 1980. In 1984, however, 81% of the respondents residing in the South favored the death penalty and 78% of the non-south favored the penalty.

HYPOTHESES

Our review of the literature in the preceding pages has shown that public opinion polls focusing on capital punishment reveal that public support for the death penalty has increased dramatically over the past few years. Empirical analyses of these data have shown, however, that increased public support for the death penalty results from an increase in the environmental salience of the crime problem affecting people's fear of criminal victimization, and that harsher punitive sanctions reflect people's idea of punishment as an effective means of controlling criminal behavior and thus lower escalating rates of crime. A logical deduction from these findings is that the American public views the growing crime problem as posing a real threat to their social well-being. Empirical analyses show, however, that people view the problem of crime as involving black-white relations (Taylor, et al., 1979; Stinchcombe, et al., 1980). It follows, then, that black persons are viewed as contributing significantly to the problem of crime. It has also been argued that racial prejudice is part of a set of attitudes and beliefs (ideology) which act to justify people's opinions about salient social problems. If white persons believe that black criminality substantially adds to the growing problem of crime, white public support toward the death penalty should be substantively imbued with racial prejudice. A reasonable interpretation of such a finding is that whites consider blacks as posing a threat to their social well-being, and that the death penalty represents a pragmatic solution to that problem.

Given our review of the literature in this chapter, we will examine the following hypotheses:

H_1:   Racially prejudiced persons are more likely to favor the death penalty than persons who are not racially prejudiced.

H_2:   Older people favor the death penalty more than younger people.

H_3:   Males favor the death penalty more than females.

H_4:   A persons' educational attainment is inversely associated with his/her support of the death penalty.

H_5:   Persons residing in the southern region of the United States are more likely to favor the death penalty than people residing in other regions of the country.

H_6:   Persons who fear criminal victimization are more likely to favor the death penalty than people who do not fear criminal victimization.

DATA AND METHOD OF ANALYSIS

Our analyses in this chapter are based on national surveys conducted by the National Opinion Research Center (NORC) 1984 General Social Survey (GSS). The 1984 (N=1473) collection employed a full probability sample of household clusters (Davis and Smith, 1986:371-381). The universe sample in 1984 was composed of noninstitutionalized English-speaking persons 18 years of age and older, who resided within the continental United States. The NORC reports a response rate of .786 for the survey year 1984.

A racism scale was constructed from seven race relation questions asked in the 1984 survey. The selection of the race relation questions used to create the racism scale was based upon a factor analysis of race relation questions asked in the 1984 survey. Table 5-1 shows that there is a very strong relationship network between the several variables labeled: RACMAR, RACDIN, RACSEG, RACOPEN, RACSCHOL, RACPUSH, AND RACHOME. All of these variables have the highest factor loadings on the first factor (FACTOR1).

Table 5-1

Factor Structure (Correlations) of Race Relations Questions*

Variable	Factor 1	Factor 2	Factor 3
RACMAR	.63405		
RACDIN	.57256		
RACPUSH	.61159		
RACOPEN	.76862		
RACSCHOL	.54462		
RACLIVE			.56174
RACHOME	.30688		
RACCHURH			.15115
SPKRAC		.62379	
LIBRAC		.77942	

* Oblique rotation

Source: Davis, James A. and Tom W. Smith. (1986). <u>General Social Survey, 1972-1986</u>. Chicago, IL: National Opinion Research Center.

The following questions were used to create the racism scale:

(1) "Do you think there should be laws against marriages between (Negroes/Blacks) and whites?" [RACMAR]

(2) "How strongly would you object if a member of your family wanted to bring a (Negro/Black) friend home to dinner?" [RACDIN]

(3) "(Negroes/Blacks) shouldn't push themselves where they're not wanted." [RACPUSH]

(4) "White people have a right to keep (Negroes/Blacks) out of their neighborhoods if they want to, and (Negroes/Blacks) should respect that right." [RACSEG]

(5) "Suppose there is a community-wide vote on the general housing issue. There are two possible laws to vote on. Which law would you vote for? One law says that a homeowner can decide for himself whom to sell his house to, even if he prefers not to sell to (Negroes/Blacks). The second law says that a home owner cannot refuse to sell to someone because of their race or color." [RACOPEN]

(6) "Do you think white students and (Negro/Black) students should go to the same schools or to separate schools." [RACSCHOL]

(7) "During the last few years, has anyone in your family brought a friend who was a (Negro/Black) home for dinner." [RACHOME]

The preceding race relation questions are assumed to provide a reasonable measure of prejudicial attitudes of whites toward blacks because these questions strive to tap the "superiority" of whites over blacks.   That is, these questions basically ask whether the respondent would discriminate against blacks if given the opportunity to do so. In addition, since most of these questions have been employed as empirical measures of prejudicial attitudes of whites toward blacks in previous research, one may assume that their validity has been operationally substantiated. (See Hyman and Sheatsley, 1965; Sheatsley, 1966; Greeley and Sheatsley, 1971; Taylor, et al., 1978; Case and Greeley, 1985a, 1985b; Stinchcombe, et al., 1980.)

The methodology employed to create the racism scale entailed a two step process. First, the race relation questions were recoded so that positive responses were coded "O" and negative responses were coded "1." Secondly, the values of these seven variables were added together. (See Nie et al., 1975:97.) The racism scale, as a result, has possible response categories from 0 to 7, with a score of 0 representing the most racially prejudiced response category. A statistical test of reliability conducted on the racism scale revealed a reasonably strong item alpha coefficient of .781. The alpha coefficient is based upon the correlation matrix presented in Table 5-2.

Table 5-2

Correlation Matrix of Race Relation Questions

	RACMAR	RACDIN	RACPUSH	RACSEG	RACOPEN	RACSCHOL
RACDIN	.37647*					
	.0001**					
	(1187)***					
RACPUSH	.34282	.24539				
	.0001	.0001				
	(1167)	(1201)				
RACSEG	.41422	.34260	.35401			
	.0001	.0001	.0001			
	(1167)	(1206)	(1199)			
RACOPEN	.23550	.20827	.21679	.33742		
	.0001	.0001	.0001	.0001		
	(1159)	(1195)	(1186)	(1188)		
RACSCHOL	.37008	.32115	.20910	.36078	.20316	
	.0001	.0001	.0001	.0001	.0001	
	(1170)	(1209)	(1196)	(1201)	(1188)	
RACHOME	.18645	.20425	.23750	.20895	.13504	.09639
	.0001	.0001	.0001	.0001	.0001	.0001
	(1186)	(1225)	(1212)	(1213)	(1204)	(1217)

*   Pearson correlation coefficient
**   Probability factor
***   Number of observations

To conform to the criteria in log-linear regression analysis that the number of cases (observations) must be at least five times the number of cells in the table (Hederson, 1987), it was necessary to recode the sociodemographic variables into dichotomous responses in order to lessen the likelihood that cells would contain zero observations. The variable age was recoded into two categories - those persons who are 39 years of age and younger comprise one category, and those persons 40 years of age and older constitute the other category. Despite this rudimentary coding technique, the distinctiveness of each category still conforms to Ryder's (1965) idea that period events influence people's political and social attitudes. According to Ryder, it is the experiences, forces, ideas, and meanings that contribute to an individual's social and cultural environment. To an extent, these entities are defined by the era in which the process of socialization is undergone.

The method of data analysis used in this study is logistic (log-linear) regression. Each hierarchical model is described as a combination of main (direct) and interaction effects of the independent variables on the dependent variable. Models are compared on the basis of their "goodness of fit" (likelihood ratio chi-square statistic and degrees of freedom) to the observed data. Comparing hierarchical models entails contrasting the degree of chi-square improvement of the fit of a model to an alternative model. That is, each direct and interaction effect is considered to improve the fit of the alternative model when the direct and/or interaction effects show an improvement of at least a 3.84 chi-square and a probability of less than or equal to .05 (95% level of confidence). All tests for significant direct and/or interaction effects are one degree of freedom tests. A "preferred model" is rendered when a particular model cannot be significantly improved upon at the .05 level of probability by including additional effects. Duncan and Duncan (1978) explain that the preferred model must (1) provide a satisfactory fit of the data, and that residual variation in the data is attributed to sampling error; (2) include the significant effects; and (3) represent the data in a parsimonious fashion (See Knoke and Burke, 1978.)

SELECTION OF PREFERRED MODEL

Tables 5-3 through 5-18 summarize the comparison of models of logit regression of responses to favoring the death penalty for persons convicted of murder (the dependent variable) on the effects of racial prejudice, age, sex, level of educational attainment, geographical region in which the respondent resides, and whether the respondent fears criminal victimization (the independent variables).

Table 5-3 specifically shows the analysis of individual parameters of the direct effects of the independent variables on the likelihood of favoring of the death peanlty. As noted in the table, the direct effect of racial prejudice, age, and sex are statistically significant since the chi-square values for these main effects exceed 3.84 and the probability factors are below or equal to .05 (the 95% level of confidence). The direct effects of education, region, and fear of criminal victimization are not statistically significant because the chi-square values for these three effects are below 3.84 and the probability factors exceed .05. This means that these effects do not significantly contribute to the overall fit of the main effects model, whereas the inclusion of the direct effects of racial prejudice, age, and sex do significantly contribute to the overall fit of the main effects model presented in the table.

Table 5-3

Direct of Effects of Racism, Age, Sex, Education, Region and
Fear on the Likelihood that the Respondent Favors the Death Penalty

Effect	Parameter Estimate	Standard Error	Chi-Square	Probability of the Null Hypotheis
Intercept	2.428	.332	53.49	.000
Racism	-0.115	.050	5.32	.021
Age	-0.464	.174	7.05	.007
Sex	-0.635	.174	13.18	.000
Education	0.098	.168	.34	.558
Region	0.110	.174	.40	.527
Fear	-0.202	.171	1.38	.239

Tables 5-4 through 5-19 summarize tests of the possible interaction effects of the independent variables on favoring capital punishment. The tables show that only the interaction effects of racial prejudice and education are statistically significant at the 95% level of confidence. Table 5-4 shows that the racial prejudice by age interaction reveals a chi-square value of 6.25 with a probability factor of .012 for one degree of freedom, and Table 5-6 shows that the racial prejudice by education interaction effects has a chi-square value of 9.27 with a probability factor of .002 for one degree of freedom. The remaining tables show that none of the other interaction effects are statistically significant and, therefore, do not improve the fit of the main effects model to the data. Thus, the "preferred model" cannot contain these interaction effects because these interaction effects do not significantly improve the fit of the model to the data.

Table 5-4

Interaction Effect of Racism by Age on the
Likelihood that the Respondent Favors the Death Penalty

Effect	Parameter Estimate	Standard Error	Chi-Square	Probability of the Null Hypotheis
Intercept	3.016	.424	50.48	.000
Racism	-0.232	.070	10.78	.001
Age	-1.491	.451	10.90	.001
Sex	-0.629	.175	12.85	.000
Education	0.123	.169	.53	.467
Region	0.109	.174	.39	.529
Fear	-0.210	.172	1.48	.223
Racism-Age	0.241	.096	6.25	.012

Table 5-5

Interaction Effect of Racism by Sex on the
Likelihood that the Respondent Favors the Death Penalty

Effect	Parameter Estimate	Standard Error	Chi-Square	Probability of the Null Hypotheis
Intercept	2.853	.440	41.86	.000
Racism	-0.208	.078	6.99	.008
Age	-0.455	.174	6.77	.009
Sex	-1.295	.461	7.89	.005
Education	0.100	.168	.35	.552
Region	0.126	.175	.52	.470
Fear	-0.209	.172	1.49	.222
Racism-Sex	0.144	.092	2.46	.117

Table 5-6

Interaction Effect of Racism by Education on the
Likelihood that the Respondent Favors the Death Penalty

Effect	Parameter Estimate	Standard Error	Chi-Square	Probability of the Null Hypotheis
Intercept	2.028	.351	33.38	.000
Racism	-0.016	.058	0.08	.783
Age	-0.448	.176	6.43	.012
Sex	-0.641	.175	13.28	.000
Education	1.748	.584	8.94	.002
Region	0.137	.175	.61	.434
Fear	-0.196	.172	1.29	.256
Racism-Educ	-0.332	.109	9.27	.002

Table 5-7

Interaction Effect of Racism by Region on the
Likelihood that the Respondent Favors the Death Penalty

Effect	Parameter Estimate	Standard Error	Chi-Square	Probability of the Null Hypotheis
Intercept	2.570	.373	47.30	.000
Racism	-0.144	.061	5.64	.017
Age	-0.470	.174	7.24	.007
Sex	-0.630	.175	12.95	.000
Education	0.097	.168	.33	.563
Region	0.220	.421	.28	.599
Fear	-0.206	.172	1.43	.231
Racism-Region	0.078	.091	.74	.389

Table 5-8

Interaction Effect of Racism by Fear on the
Likelihood that the Respondent Favors the Death Penalty

Effect	Parameter Estimate	Standard Error	Chi-Square	Probability of the Null Hypotheis
Intercept	2.207	.402	30.03	.000
Racism	-0.067	.071	.90	.343
Age	-0.458	.175	6.85	.008
Sex	-0.630	.175	12.95	.000
Education	0.101	.168	.37	.545
Region	0.119	.175	.47	.493
Fear	0.167	.429	.15	.696
Racism-Fear	-0.082	.087	.88	.348

Table 5-9

Interaction Effect of Age by Sex on the
Likelihood that the Respondent Favors the Death Penalty

Effect	Parameter Estimate	Standard Error	Chi-Square	Probability of the Null Hypotheis
Intercept	2.304	.337	46.70	.000
Racism	-0.116	.050	5.34	.020
Age	-0.062	.283	.05	.826
Sex	-0.416	.208	3.99	.045
Education	0.083	.168	.25	.619
Region	0.134	.175	.59	.443
Fear	-0.218	.173	1.60	.206
Age-Sex	-0.626	.341	3.37	.066

Table 5-10

Interaction Effect of Age by Educ on the
Likelihood that the Respondent Favors the Death Penalty

Effect	Parameter Estimate	Standard Error	Chi-Square	Probability of the Null Hypotheis
Intercept	2.558	.341	56.08	.000
Racism	-0.119	.050	5.58	.018
Age	-0.696	.213	10.69	.001
Sex	-0.628	.175	12.84	.000
Education	-0.108	.200	.29	.588
Region	0.120	.174	.48	.490
Fear	-0.220	.172	1.64	.203
Age-Educ	0.698	.364	3.67	.055

Table 5-11

Interaction Effect of Age by Region on the
Likelihood that the Respondent Favors the Death Penalty

Effect	Parameter Estimate	Standard Error	Chi-Square	Probability of the Null Hypotheis
Intercept	2.392	.333	51.35	.000
Racism	-0.116	.050	5.39	.020
Age	-0.356	.202	3.10	.078
Sex	-0.623	.175	12.63	.000
Education	-0.092	.168	.30	.581
Region	0.255	.224	1.30	.254
Fear	-0.205	.172	1.42	.233
Age-Region	-0.373	.349	1.14	.289

Table 5-12

Interaction Effect of Age by Fear on the
Likelihood that the Respondent Favors the Death Penalty

Effect	Parameter Estimate	Standard Error	Chi-Square	Probability of the Null Hypotheis
Intercept	2.526	.343	54.04	.000
Racism	-0.115	.050	5.32	.021
Age	-0.700	.258	7.33	.006
Sex	-0.625	.174	12.81	.000
Education	0.084	.168	.25	.617
Region	0.120	.174	.47	.492
Fear	-0.354	.213	2.77	.096
Age-Fear	0.403	.326	1.53	.215

Table 5-13

Interaction Effect of Sex by Educ on the
Likelihood that the Respondent Favors the Death Penalty

Effect	Parameter Estimate	Standard Error	Chi-Square	Probability of the Null Hypotheis
Intercept	2.423	.341	50.41	.000
Racism	-0.115	.050	5.33	.021
Age	-0.464	.175	7.05	.007
Sex	-0.626	.221	7.98	.004
Education	0.111	.269	.17	.677
Region	0.110	.174	.40	.528
Fear	-0.202	.171	1.38	.239
Sex-Educ	0.403	.326	1.53	.215

Table 5-14

Interaction Effect of Sex by Region on the
Likelihood that the Respondent Favors the Death Penalty

Effect	Parameter Estimate	Standard Error	Chi-Square	Probability of the Null Hypotheis
Intercept	2.485	.340	53.41	.000
Racism	-0.114	.050	5.23	.022
Age	-0.474	.175	7.32	.006
Sex	-0.722	.204	12.53	.000
Education	0.096	.168	.33	.565
Region	-0.081	.282	.08	.771
Fear	-0.202	.171	1.39	.238
Sex-Region	0.301	.353	.73	.394

Table 5-15

Interaction Effect of Sex by Fear on the
Likelihood that the Respondent Favors the Death Penalty

Effect	Parameter Estimate	Standard Error	Chi-Square	Probability of the Null Hypotheis
Intercept	2.082	.410	25.71	.000
Racism	-0.114	.050	5.24	.022
Age	-0.469	.174	7.21	.007
Sex	-0.238	.335	.50	.478
Education	0.100	.168	.36	.550
Region	-0.116	.174	.45	.503
Fear	-0.203	.340	.36	.550
Sex-Fear	-0.523	.390	1.80	.179

Table 5-16

Interaction Effect of Educ by Region on the
Likelihood that the Respondent Favors the Death Penalty

Effect	Parameter Estimate	Standard Error	Chi-Square	Probability of the Null Hypotheis
Intercept	2.506	.337	55.03	.000
Racism	-0.120	.050	5.71	.016
Age	-0.460	.174	6.95	.008
Sex	-0.635	.175	13.16	.000
Education	0.029	.191	.02	.877
Region	-0.085	.222	.15	.702
Fear	-0.207	.172	1.46	.227
Educ-Region	-0.523	.390	1.80	.179

Table 5-17

Interaction Effect of Educ by Fear on the
Likelihood that the Respondent Favors the Death Penalty

Effect	Parameter Estimate	Standard Error	Chi-Square	Probability of the Null Hypotheis
Intercept	2.337	.345	45.87	.000
Racism	-0.113	.050	5.14	.023
Age	-0.449	.175	6.56	.010
Sex	-0.632	.175	13.07	.000
Education	0.080	.258	1.17	.279
Region	0.116	.174	.44	.505
Fear	-0.077	.217	.13	.721
Educ-Fear	-0.298	.321	.87	.352

Table 5-18

Interaction Effect of Region by Fear on the
Likelihood that the Respondent Favors the Death Penalty

Effect	Parameter Estimate	Standard Error	Chi-Square	Probability of the Null Hypotheis
Intercept	2.441	.339	51.59	.000
Racism	-0.115	.050	5.34	.020
Age	-0.463	.174	7.02	.008
Sex	-0.635	.174	13.19	.000
Education	0.098	.168	.34	.559
Region	0.075	.260	.08	.773
Fear	-0.220	.200	1.21	.271
Region-Fear	0.062	.344	.03	.856

Table 5-19

Interaction Effects of Racism-Age and Racism-Educ on the
Likelihood that the Respondent Favors the Death Penalty

Effect	Parameter Estimate	Standard Error	Chi-Square	Probability of the Null Hypotheis
Intercept	2.514	.455	30.51	.000
Racism	-0.115	.050	1.99	.158
Age	-0.198	.456	6.90	.008
Sex	-0.637	.176	13.08	.000
Education	1.517	.587	6.67	.009
Region	0.128	.175	.54	.463
Fear	-0.206	.173	1.41	.234
Racism-Age	0.176	.098	3.24	.071
Racism-Educ	-0.281	.110	6.47	.011

To determine whether both of the statistically significant interaction effects of racial prejudice by age and racial prejudice by education must be included in the main effects model presented in Table 5-3, these interactions are tested simultaneously. Table 5-19 represents the test of these two interaction effects. In Table 5-19 one can observe that the racial prejudice by age interaction **does not** statistically improve the fit of the model to the data. Consequently, that interaction effect is deleted from the model. Therefore, the model which best fits the data is that model which contains the direct effects of racial prejudice, age, and sex on the likelihood of favoring the death penalty, and the interaction effect of racial prejudice by education on the likelihood of favoring the death penalty.

FINDINGS

Table 5-4 represents the parameter estimates of the direct effects of racial prejudice, age, and sex, and Table 5-6 shows the parameter estimates of the racial prejudice by education interaction effect contained within the preferred model. Taken together, these statistically significant direct effects and the one interaction effect comprise the "preferred model." Parameter estimates are the amount by which the likelihood that the respondent favors the death penalty is increased or lowered for each increment of increase in that factor.

RACISM EFFECT

Table 5-4 shows that those respondents who favor the death penalty are also more likely to be racially prejudiced. The table shows that the log-odds of a respondent favoring the death penalty decreases by .115 for respondents who are **not** racially prejudice. Or, in other words, the likelihood that a respondent who is racially prejudiced and favors the death penalty is increased by .115 log-odds over a respondent who is not racially prejudiced and favors the death penalty. [As noted, the racial prejudice scale is coded from "0" to "7" with a higher score on the racial prejudice scale representing less racial prejudice. That is, the higher the score on racial prejudice the more likely the respondent favors the death penalty.]

AGE EFFECT

The effect of age on favoring the death penalty is that the likelihood of a respondent favoring the death penalty is decreased by .464 log-odds for respondents who are in older cohorts. This effect basically means that people who are older are less likely to favor the death penalty than people who are younger cohorts.

SEX EFFECT

Table 5-4 also shows that the effect of sex on favoring the death penalty is such that a respondent who favors the death penalty is decreased by .635 log-odds for respondents who are female. This finding means that females are less likely to favor the death penalty than males.

RACIAL PREJUDICE/EDUCATION INTERACTION

Table 5-6 shows that those respondents who favor the death penalty and who are college educated are less likely to be racially prejudiced and favor the death penalty than are people who are not college educated. That is, the effect of racial prejudice and favoring the death penalty is diminished by .102 log-odds over those people who favor the death penalty and are not college educated.

DISCUSSION

The most important result of our study is the statistically significant association between racial prejudice and public support for teh death penalty. The finding shows that people who are racially prejudiced are significantly more likely to favor the death penalty than people who are not racially prejudiced. This finding tends to confirm the Stinchcombe (1980) finding that a statistically significant relationship exists between public attitudes toward the death penalty ("punitiveness") and public sentiment concerning the equal treatment of blacks ("liberalism").

Our findings also show that younger people are more likely to favor the death penalty than are older people. This finding does not support previous empirical findings which have shown that younger cohorts are less likely to favor capital punishment than older cohorts. From this finding, however, it cannot be conclusively argued that younger cohorts of people hve been any less fervently socialized to a punitive ideology than have their older counterparts. As such, our results have shown that the relationship between racial prejudice and age is not statistically significant. This finding may be interpreted to mean that the punitive attitudes of both the young and the old have become equally consistent with a racist ideology. That is, for both younger and older people, racial prejudice is part of a set of attitudes and beliefs by which people justify their opinions concerning the death penalty. While it is assumed that younger cohorts of people are more egalitarian because they have been socialized in a cultural environment that reflects more equal treatment of minorities, our results suggest that as a society we may formally recognize and teach the young that blacks are to be treated equally, but we still socialize them to a racist ideology. Based on our findings, one could speculate that the young are being socialized to the idea that blacks are to blame for society's evils (crime) and that appropriate punishment should reflect that social-political idea (racism).

Our results have also shown that a respondent's level of educational attainment has a statistically significant effect on his/her racist punitive attitudes. This finding specifically shows that increased levels of educational attainment tend to diminish the effects of racial prejudice on public support for capital punishment. This finding, however, tends to contradict the Sears, et al. (1975) argument that basic social-political values are highly resistant to change. An increase in peoples' knowledge about their cultural environment (a result of formal education) appears to thwart the premises upon which a racist punitive ideology is predicated. While our results have shown that formal education has a significant impact on racist punitive attitudes, our findings further show that education **does not** directly effect public support for the death penalty. This finding, however, does not support several public opiinion polls which show that people with higher levels of educational attainment are less supportive of the death penalty than people with lower levels of education.

Our results also show that males and females continue to systematically differ in their punitive attitudes. Our findings, however, do not show that males and females differ across categories of the other sociodemographic variables. For example, while males are considerably more likely to favor the death penalty than are females, our findings show that males and females (e.g., gender) cannot be distinguished in their racist punitive attitudes. That is, there is no statistically significant interaction of racial prejudice by sex and public support for the death penalty. The finding that males and females do not systematically vary in relation to racist punitive attitudes would appear to mean that both males and females are socialized equally well to a racist punitive ideology.

As we noted, in this chapter, several studies have shown that a person's perception of increasing crime rates is directly associated with his/her fear of criminal victimization and a willingness to employ punishment as a response to criminality. The results of the present analysis, however, are unable to confirm this contention. Our analysis has shown that there is no statistically significant relationship between fear of criminal victimization and support for the death penalty. This finding indicates that the fear of criminal victimization neither increases nor decreases the likelihood that people will favor the death penalty for persons convicted of murder. This is not to argue, however, that there is no effect of fear of criminal victimization on the likelihood of favoring the death penalty. Table 5-3, in fact, shows that the likelihood that respondents favor the death penalty is decreased by .202 log-odds for respondents who do not fear criminal victimization. In other words, people who fear criminal victimization are also more likely to favor the death penalty. However, given this sample of respondents, this interaction effect is not statistically significant and, therefore, the null hypothesis that this effect is not subject to random sample error must be rejected.

An equally important finding is that there is no statistically significant interaction effect of fear of criminal victimization by racial prejudice on the likelihood that respondents favor the death penalty. Once again, however, it cannot be argued that there is no interaction effect between the variables, but rather, that the relationship is not statistically significant. Table 5-8 specifically shows that a respondent who is not racially prejudiced and does not fear criminal victimization is less likely to favor the death penalty by .082 log-odds. In other words, a person who is racially prejudiced and fears criminal victimization is more likely to favor the death penalty. That is, fear of criminal victimization increases the likelihood that a racially prejudiced respondent favors the death penalty. This effect, however, is statistically unreliable.

Coupled with the evidence of racial discrimination in the application of the death penalty against blacks provided in Chapter Three, the finding that white racial attitudes significantly influence public support for the death penalty supports empirical evidence that racial oppression is institutionalized within the American criminal justice system. As noted, Turner, et. al. (1984) point out that racial oppression becomes institutionalized when discriminatory acts are built into social structures and legitimated by cultural beliefs. The finding that racial prejudice influences public attitudes toward the death penalty shows that cultural beliefs toward punitiveness are predicated upon the same racist ideology as are the structural arrangements of the legal system which act to discriminate against blacks in imposing capital punishment. This means that race has become a political identity to the extent that race defines the way in which black prisoners are to be treated by the state.

Secondly, the finding that racial prejudice significantly influences white public support for the death penalty means that the values and ideas of a racist ideology sanction discretionary use of the death penalty against black persons. Essentially, the death penalty is sanctioned by the white majority partly as a mechanism by which to protect itself from black persons who are perceived as posing a threat to the social well-being of the white majority. In this sense, the death penalty amounts to a very effective instrument by which the white majority can exert its power over the black subordinate group. The death penalty also acts to give warning to the black minority that infringement upon the social interests of the white majority will not be tolerated. The finding that the attitudes of younger and older whites toward the death penalty are equally imbued with racial prejudice indicates that the racist ideology is precipitated through group norms denoting that black persons significantly contribute to the problem of crime and that the death penalty is an appropriate means of controlling black criminality.

CONCLUDING REMARKS

Our major objective in this chapter has been to empirically evaluate the significance of the relationship between racism and public sentiment toward the death penalty. It has been shown that white racist attitudes measurably influence public support for the death penalty. Our findings have shown that during periods of increased public concern over the growing problem of crime, it is the younger cohorts of people who express the harshest punitive attitudes. Our results probably illustrate the extent to which younger cohorts are affected by period events within the social environment. The finding that younger and older cohorts of respondents are equally defined by racist punitive attitudes contradicts the idea that younger people are socialized to a more egalitarian cultural environment. Our results have also been shown that while females tend to favor the death penalty less than males, both females and males have been socialized equally well to the same racial ideology. More importantly, this study has shown that racism is still an integral part of American society in that at least part of the white majority not only regards blacks as posing a threat against the social well-being of whites, but that the death penalty is an appropriate means by which to protect that interest. Taken together, racial discrimination in the imposition of the death penalty toward blacks and white racist punitive attitudes toward blacks act to oppress blacks to a social position of subjugation exploitation.

PART III

THE SOCIO-CULTURAL DIMENSIONS OF RACIAL INEQUALITY: SUMMARY AND CONCLUDING STATEMENTS

CHAPTER SIX

INSTITUTIONALIZED RACIAL DISCRIMINATION
IN THE IMPOSITION OF THE DEATH PENALTY TO BLACKS:
THE UNITED STATES SUPREME COURT

In the preceding two chapters of this work we reviewed several empirical research studies that conclusively showed that in the United States the death penalty has been historically and contemporaneously applied in a discriminatory and discretionary manner against blacks. Our purpose of this chapter, however, is to briefly review those landmark decisions of the United States Supreme Court that have focused on racial discrimination in the use of the death penalty.[19] The underlying theme of this chapter is that the Supreme Court, through a variety of decisions, has sanctioned institutionalized racial discrimination in the imposition of the death penalty to blacks. Our review will illustrate that the Supreme Court has come to literally sanction racism as an ideological basis by which to impose justice in the capital sentencing of blacks in the United States.

DEATH SENTENCES

The President's Commission on Law Enforcement and Administration of Justice pointed out in 1967 that "there is [now] evidence that the imposition of the death sentence and the exercise of dispensing power by the courts ... follow discriminatory patterns. The death sentence is disproportionately imposed and carried out on the poor, the Negro, and the members of unpopular groups." Former United States Supreme Court Justice Arthur J. Goldberg argued three years later, in 1970, that capital punishment should be declared unconstitutional on the basis of the Eight and Fourteenth Amendments to the Federal Constitution because it is "highly suspect under the standards of degrading severity and wanton imposition" (Goldberg and Dershowetz, 1970:1784). It wasn't until January of 1972, that the United States Supreme Court addressed the question of racial discrimination the application of the death penalty. In **Furman v. Georgia** (1972), the Court declared that all state death penalty statutes then in effect were unconstitutional. Fifteen years later, however, in **McClesky v. Kemp** (1987) the Court held that racial discrimination in the imposition of the death penalty is constitutional and does not in fact violate defendants' Eighth and Fourteenth Amendment rights of "equal protection of the law" and against "cruel and unusual punishment."

The central debate surrounding the Court's decisions on racial discrimination in the use of the death penalty since **Furman v. Georgia** (1972) has been on the strength of empirical evidence necessary for the Court to accept the claim that racial factors do in fact strongly influence state imposition of capital punishment statues. Samuel Gross (1985) has elaborated at length on this point. It is his contention that "for years courts have rejected claims of discrimination by finding that the evidence of effects was too weak; now, in the face of mounting proof that the race of the victim plays an undeniable role in determining who is sentenced to death, they are shifting their grounds.... The new position is that the essential question is not the evidence of discrimination but its magnitude, and that even the strongest claims deserve no hearing because the quantity of racial discrimination they allege is too small" (Gross, 1985:1275).

FURMAN V. GEORGIA (1972)

Together with **Jackson v. Georgia** (1972) and **Branch v. Texas** (1972), the United States Supreme Court held by a bare majority in **Furman v. Georgia** (1972) that the imposition of the death penalty as curently administered in the United States amounted to "cruel and unusual punishment" as prohibited by the Eighth and Fourteenth Amendments. The holding not only set aside the sentences of the three defendants Furman, Branch, and Jackson, but the decision also vacated some 120 other cases coming up before the Court from some thirty-six states, and the pending executions of some 645 death row inmates in prisons throughout the nation. (See Ehrhadt et al., 1973; **Virginia Law Review**, 1972; McDonald, 1972; Note, 1973.) Galloway (1978) notes that the death penalty statues of 40 states, the District of Columbia, and the federal government were overruled as defective and unconstitutional pursuant to **Furman**.

The 5-4 decision in **Furman** contains nine different opinions with five separate one-vote opinions comprising the majority holding. While Justices Brennan and Marshall found the death penalty per se unconstitutional because it is cruel and unusual punishment pursuant to the Eighth Amendment, Justices Douglas, Stewart, and White found capital punishment not per se unconstitutional, but argued instead that capital punishment is invalid because it is applied in an arbitrary and capricious manner. Chief Justice Burger, and Associate Justices Powell, Rehnquist, and Blackmun argued that abolition of the death penalty was strictly a matter for Congress to determine.

Despite the overall importance that the racial disparity issue had on the finding in **Furman,** only five of the nine Justices approached the issued of racial discrimination in the imposition of the death penalty. Citing empirical research findings from several different studies which showed it is the poor and blacks who are more likely to suffer imposition of the death penalty than other racial or economic groups, Justice Douglas concluded that the death penalty statutes before the Court at that time were "pregnant with discrimination" (**Furman**, 1972:257). Relying on similar research findings, Justice Marshall argued that capital punishment is unconstitutional because it is "imposed discriminatorily against certain identifiable classes of people" and that it is "morally reprehensible" to American values (**Furman**, 1972:363-369). While Justice Stewart disagreed with Justices Douglas and Marshall that racial discrimination had been conclusively proven to be a factor in imposing the death penalty, he did argue, however, that the Justices "have demonstrated that, if any basis can be discerned for the selection of these few to be sentenced to die, it is the constitutionally impermissible basis of race" (**Furman**, 1972:310). Of the dissenters, Chief Justice Burger and Justice Powell mentioned the relationship between racial discrimination and use of the death penalty. While both Justices found the evidence of racial discrimination against blacks particularly valid, they believed that the proper role of the Court was not to determine public policy. Rather, such determination should be the exclusive responsibility of legislators, and not judges.

The essence of the **Furman** decision is that it represents the first attempt by the United States Supreme Court to formally recognize that the imposition of capital punishment in the United States has been systematically reserved for a select group of people - namely, blacks, the poor, and the powerless. (See the brief filed by the NAACP in **Aikens v. California**, 1972.)

Two basic facts concerning the application of the death penalty have resulted from the **Furman** decision. First, the Court recognized that the death penalty per se is not unconstitutional, but that the manner in which the penalty had been applied (discretionary and discriminatory) in the past is unconstitutional because it denies the sentenced equal protection of the law (Fourteenth Amendment) and amounts to cruel and unusual punishment (Eighth Amendment). Secondly, the Court made it clear that certain guidelines must be devised that will secure restricted discretion in remanding prisoners to death. In **Gregg**, the Court established these guidelines.

GREGG V. GEORGIA (1976)

When the **Furman** decision was first handed down by the United States Supreme Court in 1972, many scholars interpreted the finding as the abolition of capital punishment in the United States. (See Gross, 1985.) In 1976, however, the Court granted certeriori to **Gregg v. Georgia** and its two companion cases; **Proffit v. Florida**, and **Jurek v. Texas**. The leading case was **Gregg v. Georgia**. In this case, the state of Georgia provided the Court with a set of procedural safeguards designed to guide the discretion of the sentencer (judge or jury). The Georgia post-**Furman** statute provided for bifurcated trials (**Gregg**, 1976:185), defined aggravating circumstances (**Gregg**, 1976:192-195), and provided for automatic appellate review of all capital sentences (**Gregg**, 1976:204-206). It was argued in **Gregg** that bifurcated trials (one for the determination of guilt and another for rendering the appropriate punishment) would guard against irrelevant evidence influencing the sentencing decision. The Georgia statute also made it mandatory that the death penalty could not be imposed unless the jury unanimously and beyond a reasonable doubt found that the offender had aggravated the circumstances of the crime by committing one of ten listed grievances. the Georgia statute also required that the Georgia Supreme Court review the capital cases in order to "determine whether the evidence supported the jury's finding of an aggravating circumstance and whether the imposition of the death penalty was excessive or disproportionate to the penalty imposed in similar cases" (Galloway, 1978:9). In other words, the Court in **Gregg** argued that capital punishment does not necessarily amount to "cruel and unusual punishment" so long as certain procedural safeguards designed to curb arbitrary and capricious application of the death penalty are implemented. That is, the death penalty is constitutionally permissible for the crime of murder where discretion is "reasonable and controlled." (See **Jurek v. Texas**, 1976; and **Woodson v. North Carolina**, 1976; **Stanislaus Roberts v. Louisiana**, 1976; **Lockett v. Ohio**, 1978; **Spinkellink v. Wainwright**, 1979).

COKER V. GEORGIA (1977)

On June 29, 1977, the United States Supreme Court declared in **Coker** that imposition of the death penalty for the rape of an adult woman where death was not a result is "grossly disproportionate and excessive punishment" and, therefore, in violation of a defendant's Eighth Amendment protection against "cruel and unusual punishment." In terms of racial discrimination in the application of the death penalty, the **Coker** decision is not so important for what is stated in the opinion of the Court as it is for what is not considered. As noted by Gross (1976:195), "one of the most conspicuous things about the **Coker** opinion is the absence of any reference to race." **Coker** is important because seven years earlier in **Maxwell v. Bishop** (1970), the Court was presented with empirically based evidence that racial discrimination exists in the use of the death penalty against blacks convicted for rape. Despite this evidence, the Court refused to rule on the issue of racial discrimination and vacated and remanded the case on other grounds. The **habeas corpus** petition filed by Maxwell claimed that, pursuant to the Wolfgang and Reidel (1975) study, blacks convicted of rape were over seven times more likely to be sentenced to death than whites convicted of rape, and that blacks convicted of raping a white woman were some eighteen times more likely to be sentenced to death than persons in any other racial category who were convicted of rape. (See Chapter Two for a more detailed discussion of the Wolfgang and Reidel study.) The Eighth Circuit Court of Appeals, however, ignored this claim by Maxwell. The Court argued that because only some of the rape cases analyzed in the study came from the same Alabama county in which Maxwell was convicted, and because the data "do not take every variable into account," the data are too broad and too shallow for the Court to consider. (See **Maxwell**, 398 F.2d at 147.) Further, the Court held that Maxwell had failed to show that the evidence presented in the case conclusively pointed out that Maxwell's death sentence resulted from racial discrimination on the part of the jury. (See Gross and Mauro, 1986; **Moorer v. South Carolina**, 1966; Bell, 1973.) The major point here is that the Supreme Court granted certeriori to the **Maxwell** case, and therefore, was confronted with the same evidence heard by the Circuit Court of Appeals. Since the Court refused to review the issue of racial discrimination, the Court let stand the Circuit Court's holding on the issue of racial discrimination in imposition of the death penalty to defendants convicted of rape.

MCCLESKY V. KEMP (1987)

On April 22, 1987, the United States Supreme Court handed down its latest decision concerning racial discrimination in imposition of the death penalty. Associate Justice Powell delivered the opinion of the Court and was joined by Chief Justice Rehnquist, and Justices White, O'Connor, and Scalia. Justices Brennan, Blackmun, and Stevens filed dissenting opinions which Justice Marshall joined in part. The question before the Court in **McClesky** was whether a complex statistical study that indicates a risk that racial consideration enters into capital sentencing determinations...is unconstitutional under the Eighth and Fourteenth Amendments (**McClesky**, 1987:1).

The facts surrounding the case are such that McClesky, a black man, was convicted in Fulton County, Georgia, in 1978 for the murder of a white police officer during the commission of an armed robbery of a furniture store. In keeping with the Georgia death penalty statute that a jury cannot sentence a defendant to death for murder without finding beyond a reasonable doubt that the crime was aggravated by at least one of ten particular circumstances, the jury found that McClesky had committed the murder during the course of an armed robbery, and that McClesky had murdered an on-duty police officer. McClesky failed to present any mitigating evidence to the jury and was subsequently sentenced to death.

On appeal to the United States Supreme Court, McClesky claimed that the Georgia capital sentencing process is administered in a racially discriminatory manner in violation of the Eighth Amendment protection against "cruel and unusual punishment," and that the discriminatory system violates the Fourteenth Amendment guarantee to "equal protection of the law." McClesky presented the results of the Baldus study in support of his claim. From an analysis of over 2000 murder cases that occurred in Georgia during the 1970's, David C Baldus and his associates found that defendants who killed whites were sentenced to death in 11% of the cases, and that defendants who killed blacks were sentenced to death in only 1% of the cases. Baldus also found that the death penalty is imposed in 22% of the cases where the defendant was convicted of murdering a white, 8% of the cases with white defendants-white victims, 3% of the cases with white defendants-black victims, and only 1% of the cases involving black defendants and black victims resulted in capital sentences. Baldus controlled for some 230 non-racial variables and found that none of these variables could account for the racial disparities in capital sentences among the different racial combinations of defendant-victim. Baldus found that killers of whites were 4.3 times more likely to be sentenced to death than killers of blacks, and that black defendants were 1.1 times more likely to be sentenced to death than other defendants. McClesky claimed that race had, therefore, infected the administration of capital punishment in Georgia in two distinct ways. First, McClesky argued that "prisoners who murder whites are more likely to be sentenced to death than prisoners who murder blacks," and secondly, that "black murders are more likely to be sentenced to death than white murders" (McClesky, 1987:9). McClesky held that he was discriminated against by the Georgia system of imposing the death penalty because he is a black man who killed a white man.

Writing for the majority of the Court, Justice Powell held that the Baldus study does not prove that the administration of the Georgia capital punishment system violates the Equal Protection Clause of the Fourteenth Amendment or the Eighth Amendment protection against cruel and unusual punishment. The Court held that "a defendant who alleges an equal protection violation has the burden of proving 'the existence of purposeful discrimination,'" and that "the purposeful discrimination had a discriminatory effect on him." That is, the Court believed that McClesky must prove that the jury in his particular case acted with a discriminatory purpose - that to establish only that a "pattern" of racial discrimination in imposing the death penalty to select group of defendants is not sufficient to support a claim of constitutional viiolation of equal protection of the law. The Court further pointed out that McClesky's claim that evidence of racial discrimination supports a violation of the Eighth Amendment safeguard against cruel and unusual punishment also fails because McClesky "cannot prove a constitutuional violation by demonstrating the other defendants who may be similarly situated did not receive the death penalty." The Georgia sentencing procedures were found by the Court to be sufficient in adequately focusing discretion "on the particularized nature of the crime and the particularized characteristics of the individual defendant," and that it cannot, therefore, be presumed that McClesky's death sentence was "wantonly and freakishly" imposed. That is, McClesky's death sentence was not found to be disproportionate in respect to the Eighth Amendment.

The essence of the Court's holding in McClesky is that there is an acceptable standard of risk for racial discrimination in the imposition of the death penalty. The Court held that the Baldus study simply shows that a discrepancy appears to correlate with race in imposing death sentences, but the "statistics do not prove that race enters into any capital sentencing decisions or that race was a factor in petitioners cases." Lastly, the Court was also concerned that a finding for the defendant in this case would open other claims that "could be extended to apply to other types of penalties and to claims based on unexplained discrepancies correlating to membership in other minority groups and even to gender."

To Justices Brennan, Marshall, Blackmun, and Stevens, "McClesky has clearly demonstrated that his death sentence was imposed in violation of the Eighth and Fourteenth Amendments," and that "[n]othing could convey more powerfully the intractable reality of the death penalty: 'that the effort to eliminate arbitrariness in the infliction of that ultimate sanction is so plainly doomed to failure that it - and the death penalty - must be abandoned altogether" (McClesky, 1987:39). The dissenters specifically argued that whether McClesky can prove racial discrimination in his particular case is totally irrelevant in evaluating McClesky's claim of a constitutional violation. The Justices pointed out that the Court has long recognized that the establishment of a "pattern" of substantial risk of arbitrary and capricious capital sentencing suffices for a claim of unconstitutionality.

The dissenting Justices also called into question the effectiveness of the statutory safeguards designed to curb discretionary use of the death penalty. Justice Brennan specifically argued that "[w]hile we may hope that a model of procedural fairness [as that established in Gregg] will curb the influence of race on sentencing, 'we cannot simply assume that the model works as intended; we must critique its performance in terms of its results'" (McClesky, 1987:19-20).

The dissenting Justices were particularly dismayed by the Court's fear that finding McClesky's clsim sufficient would "open the door to widespread challenges to all aspects of criminal sentencing." To Justice Brennan, the Court's rejection of McClesky's evidence of racial discrimination in imposition of the death penalty on the basis that it would open further challenges to criminal sentencing "is to ignore both the qualitatively different character of the death penalty and the particular repugnance of racial discrimination..." (**McClesky**, 1987:21-22).

Justice Blackmun found that McClesky had in fact established a **prima facie** case of purposeful discrimination "by showing that the totality of the relevant facts gives rise to an inference of discriminatory purpose," and thus the burden of proving that discrimination was not purposeful shifts to the prosecution. In accordance with **Batson v. Kentucky** (1986) and **Castaneda v. Partida** (1977), Justice Blackmun argued that McClesky (1) is a member of a group "that is a recognizable, distinct class, singled out for different treatment," (2) he has made "a showing of a substantial degree of differential treatment," and (3) that he has established that "the allegedly discriminatory procedure is susceptible to abuse or is not racially neutral."

CONCLUDING REMARKS

Our brief review of the most recent United States Supreme Court cases concerning racial discrimination in the imposition of the death penalty has shown that a number of issues have been resolved about the manner in which the death penalty can be imputed to capital offenders. In **Furman**, the Court officially denounced racial discrimination in the use of the death penalty as unconstitutional. While the Court held that the death penalty itself does not per se amount to cruel and unusual punishment, discriminatory and discretionary application of the penalty to a selected group of prisoners does, however, violate the Fourteenth Amendment provision for equal protection of the law and the Eighth Amendment safeguard against cruel and unusual punishment.

Gregg established that the death penalty is reserved as a punishment for perpetrating a criminal homicide (**Coker**), but that the penalty must not involve unnecessary or wanton infliction of pain, be disproportionate to the crime committed, and it must serve some penological purpose (e.g., retribution or deterrence). The Court has established that the imposition of the death penalty must involve sufficient provisions designed to eliminate unbridled discretion of the penalty and to make it subject to appellate review. The provisions guiding the application of the death penalty to capital offenders must further allow for the mitigation of the circumstances of the offender's character, past criminal record, and circumstances of the crime itself.

As we have suggested in Chapter Two, however, the wrongs of racial prejudice, racial inequality, and caprice in the imposition of the death penalty have **not** been abolished by the procedural safeguards established in **Gregg**. Capital punishment continues to be imposed in a wanton and freakish and discriminatory manner against black criminal defendants. As Goodman (1987:499) has explained, "the sentencer's choice between life and death increasingly appears inchoate and uncontrollable, a decision more visceral than cerebral."

Empirically based evidenced that racial discrimination continues to influence the imposition of the death penalty has literally been ignored by the Court (**McClesky**). The proposed safeguards that surround the imposition of the death penalty amount to no safeguards at all. The only substantive conclusion that can be drawn from our review is that the Court has moved from a position of formally recognizing that imposition of the death penalty is imbued with racial prejudice (**Furman**), to a position of sanctioning racial prejudice as a cost of imposing the penalty (**McClesky**). It appears from the cases handed down from the Court that racism is a legitimate penological doctrine. For the advocates of racial and ethnic equality, the death penalty cannot be morally justified on the premise that racial oppression, subjugation, and social subservience are legitimate liabilities of maintaining social order. Social order under these circumstances amounts to social order predicated upon a racist ideology.

CHAPTER SEVEN

THE DEATH PENALTY AS A
MECHANISM OF SOCIAL CONTROL OF BLACKS:
CONCLUDING OBSERVATIONS

We have noted in the preceding chapters that the socio-cultural dynamics of racial oppression involve a complex interplay between social structure and cultural beliefs. We have argued, pursuant to Turner, et al. (1984), that racial oppression occurs when discriminatory acts are built into social structures (institutionalized) and when these discriminatory acts are legitimized or sanctioned by cultural beliefs and legal codes. As such, racial oppression takes on two dimensions: a physical/structural dimension, wherein the structural arrangements of social institutions act to physically control members of a "perceived" inferior group through discriminatory actions; and a socio-cultural dimension, whereby the cultural (prejudicial) beliefs and thte statutory (legal) requirements act to lesitimate or sanction these physical controls of the subordinate group. The purpose of this chapter is to argue that these two dimensions of racial oppression have been clearly shown to characterize racial discrimination in the imposition of the death penalty to blacks. As a result, capital punishment in the United States is an oppressive mechanism utilized by the dominant white group in the society to help American blacks relegated to a subservient and subjugated social position.

THE CONTEXT

Chapters Three and Four have conclusively shown that the death penalty has been dispropor-tionately imposed on black prisoners for the crimes of rape and murder. Specifically, Chapter Three is a review and summary of some of the major empirically based studies conducted on the disproportionate use of the death penalty to blacks. In the pre-**Furman** studies, the chapter points out that the death penalty has been systematically applied to black defendants in a discretionary and discriminatory manner. Several studies have also been conducted on racial discrimination in the imposition of capital punishment during the interim period between the **Furman** and the **Gregg** decisions. These studies have shown that despite the declaration of the United States Supreme Court in **Furman** that the discriminatory and discretionary manner in which the death penalty has been applied is blatantly unconstitutional, these studies show that the decision had little or no effect on diminishing the extent to which black capital offenders were subjugated to racial discrimination in imposing the death penalty. Black defendants with white victims were overwhelmingly convicted and sentenced to death when compared to other racial categories of defendant-victim. Lastly, several other studies conducted on the death penalty after the Court decided **Gregg** found that the procedural guidelines established in that case have essentially failed to eliminate racial disparities in capital cases. In sum, the essence of all of these empirical studies is that they show that the death penalty has and continues to be used disproportionatley against black defendants. Moreover, the death penalty is shown to have been used and continues to be used as a specific device by which to protect whites. That is, the death penalty has been more readily used against black defendants who kill or rape whites than any other racial combination of defendant-victim. These studies conclusievly show that the imposition of the death penalty amounts to individualized acts of racial discrimination, and that this pattern of discriminatorily applying the death penalty to blacks has become institutionalized within the American criminal justice system.

Secondly, the empirical analysis presented in Chapter Four shows that throughout the history of state-imposed capital punishment in the United States, black prisoners have been considerably more likely to have been executed in Southern states than non-blacks. The analysis has also shown that black prisoners have had a greater likelihood of being executed for rape than non-black prisoners. In addition, Black prisoners have been less likely to have been afforded the opportunity to appeal their capital cases to a higher tribunal. Black prisoners have also been more likely to have been executed in later years than in the earlier years covered by the study. The findings of our analysis show that black prisoners have been more likely to have been executed for the crime of rape in the Southern states than non-black prisoners. Taken together, our findings support previous research findings that provide rather persuasive evidence that the death penalty has been systematically applied in a discriminatory manner against black prisoners.

The most substantive conclusion that can be drawn from the discussion presented in Chapter Six is that the discriminatory manner in which the death penalty has, and continues, to be applied against blacks is supported (legitimated or sanctioned) by the statutory requirements of imposition of the penalty. This chapter has shown that the wrongs of racial prejudice, racial inequality, and caprice in the imposition of the death penalty have not been abolished by the Court, but rather, the latest decision of the Court is that these social wrongs are a cost of doing business (imposing the death penalty). The Court has moved from a position of formally recognizing that imposition of the death penalty is imbued with racial discrimination (**Furman**), to a position of sanctioning racial discrimination (**McClesky**).

Taken together, Chapters Four and Five have shown that cultural beliefs support, legitimate, or sanction the manner in which the death penalty has and continues to be imposed on Black Americans. Chapter Four specifically points out that lynching has been systematically used against blacks. Not only have blacks been disproportionately lynched when compared to whites, but black lynchings have entailed the most insidious forms of barbarism and torture. The rationale for the lynching of blacks has been the fear that whites have for the economic, social, and political progress that blacks began to experience during Reconstruction. The rape myth was specifically inviting to the white lynch mob because it gave credence to black lynchings that otherwise was impossible to justify. The most disheartening aspect of black lynchings in this country is that the power to execute has simply transferred from the hands of the lynch mob to the power of the state. By contrasting and comparing legal and illegal executions, we find that both forms of execution represent retributive forms of justice designed to principally thwart black criminality. However, the pervasiveness of black lynchings throughout the history of the United States dramatically illustrates the extent to which white public sentiment has sanctioned systematic execution of blacks.

To complement our discussion in Chapter Five, we have analyzed in Chapter Six the extent to which racial prejudice influences public opinion on the death penalty. Our analysis has shown that white racist attitudes measurably influence public support for the death penalty. Our analysis has shown that racism is still an integral part of American society in that the white majority not only regards blacks as posing a threat against the social well-being of whites, but that the death penalty is regarded as the appropriate means by which to protect that interest.

SYNTHESIS

The analyses and discussions presented in the preceding individual chapters show that the requirements for showing that racial oppression characterizes the imposition of the death penalty have been sastisfied. The structural dimension of racial oppression in the use of the death penalty has been shown to the extent that blacks have been systematically executed in greater numbers than other racial and ethnic groups, and that the racial disparities present in the imposition of the death penalty amount to systematic racial discrimination. In addition, the cultural dimension of racial oppression has been successfully measured. The analyses on black lynchings and public support for capital punishment show that the cultural beliefs of American society are such that discriminatory use of the death penalty is a legitimate and sanctioned (appropriate) use of the penalty because it is designed to protect the interests (social well-being) of whites. The legal codes concerning the imposition of capital punishment in the United States have also been shown to sanction discriminatory use of the death penalty.

We need to briefly return to the discussion of the Internal Colonial Model of racial and ethnic inequality presented in Chapter One. As noted, we have supplemented Barrera's understanding of the model to incorporate the idea that legal and illegal (lynching) executions increase racial tension, and thus, racial prejudice. It is our contention, as discussed in the preceding paragraph, that a system of structural discrimination in the imposition of the death penalty has been established. However, it is also our contention that while such a system of structural discrimination may exist, the underlying motivation for the establishment of such a system will solely be for the protection of interests in the white dominant group. While racial inequality can be product of any system of structural discrimination, racial inequality will only be the product of the imposition of the death penalty if the penalty is in fact disproportionately applied to a select group, and if the racial disparity of the imposition of the penalty is systematically applied to a select group specifically for the protection of the interests of the white dominant group. This is the case in the imposition of the death penalty in American society to black Americans.

OUR FINAL NOTE

The argument is often posited that the disparity in application of the death penalty among blacks and whites for murder and rape knowingly reflects differential offense rates. According to Wolfgang and Cohen (1970), however, higher levels of violent crimes committed by blacks must be attributed to the social effects of racial discrimination. They argue that "a society that places and holds certain of its citizens in condition of poverty and disadvantage with respect to occupation and education has itself created the circumstances that lead to criminal violence among the members of its oppressed minority" (1970:138). It is, therefore, the very nature of the econommic social structure of American capitalism that breeds disenfranchised groups. Basically, it is the economic, social, and political needs of the white dominant group in American society that perpetuates racial discrimination. The gross disproportion in the distribution of wealth is responsible for the spawning of prestige, power, and status. The more material wealth the dominant group acquires, the less that remains for others. The dominant group in society acquires its material wealth at the expense of the minority groups. The dominant group is better prepared than the minority group to obtain wealth because minority groups are deprived of the opportunities to education and occupation. According to Blumer (1961), the dominant group in society is taught to believe that they are entitled to certain rights and privileges, and that these rights and privileges should not be afforded to minority groups. Imposition of the death penalty throughout American history has amounted to the use of a mechanism designed to thwart a perceived minority threat, by members of the dominant group, to the favorable positions in society. In this case, the dominant and most powerful group in the United States uses the death penalty to safeguard their social, political, and economic positions from minority group infringement.

ENDNOTES

1. The internal colonial model has been widely used by social scientists to study the relative degree of inequality present in American minority groups. For examples of how the model is employed in the study of the principal minority groups of the United States society see: Native Americans - Gedicks (1985), Churchill (1985), McKenna (1981), Jacobson (1984), Bee and Gingerich 1977); Asian Americans - Kagiwada (1982); African Americans - Feagin (1986), White (1981), Hill (1980), Laguerre (1979), Staples (1975), Lieberman (1973); Mexican Americans - Martinez (1982), Morrisey (1983), Almaguer (1971), and Barrera, et al. (1972).

2. The concept of internal colonialism has been employed by numerous social scientists to examine the effects of colonialization on evey day social behavior. For a statement of the ideal ltype concept of internal colonialism, the reader is advised to consult the following: Blauner (1972), Fanon (1968), Memmi (1965).

3. The race of the offender has been omitted for 259 executions in California, for 76 executions in Colorado, for 64 executions in Illinois, for 65 executions in Massachusetts, for 34 executions in Nevada, for 12 executions in New Hampshire, for 29 executions in New York, for 1 execution in North Dakota, for 59 executions in Oregon, for 104 executions in Pennsylvania, for 1 execution in South Dakota, for 31 executions in Utah, for 21 executions in Vermont, and for 14 executions in Wyoming.

4. The District of Columbia, Ohio and Tennessee have not reported whether the offender had the capital case appealed to a higher court for 112, 343, and 125 executions, respectively.

5. Parameter estimates can defined as the amount by which the likelihood of the offender being black is increased or lowered for each increment of increase in that factor.

6. See, for example, Brearley, 1930; Myrdal, 1933; Mangum, 1940; Johnson, 1941; Allredge, 1942; Garfinkel, 1949; Johnson, 1957; Florida Civil Liberties Union, 1964; Koeninger, 1969; Wolfgang, 1972; Reidel, 1975; Bowers and Pierce, 1981; Radelet, 1981; Zeifel, 1981; Paternoster, 1983; Radelet and Vandiver, 1983; Gross and Mauro, 1984, 1989; Baldus, et al., 1980, 1983.

7. See, for example, Ohio Legislative Service Commission, 1961; Wolfgang et al., 1962; Zimring et al., 1976; Carter and Smith, 1969; **Stanford Law Review**, 1969; Bowers and Pierce, 1980; Bedau, 1964, 1965; Wolf, 1964; Gross and Mauro, 1984, 1989.

8. Lynching began in the United States as a means of maintaining social and community security from outlaws and British loyalists during the Revolutionary War (Cutler, 1905). The term **lynching** has been associated with Judge Charles Lynch, a Quaker and House of Burgesses representative, who was chief magistrate of an extra-legal court in what is now called Lynchburg, Virginia. Since the only legal cour was some 200 miles from Lynchburg, Judge Lynch's court was the central autority within the region. Despite the illegality of Lynch's court, it did, however, conform to established standards of law and legal procedures. It appears that Judge Lynch was dedicated to preserving individual rights. Each defendant who was brought before Lynch was given the opportunity to defend himself. Punishment was usually in the form of lashings or whippings, but tar and feathering and hanging by the thumbs were also used. Only rarely was a defendant executed. Other states readily adopted similar courts in the post-Revolutionary era. However, by about 1800 adherence to democratic principles of criminal justice by these courts quickly diminished, and lynching had become identified with the

execution of an accused person at the hands of court delegates. Junge Lynch became known as the notorious "hanging judge."

9. It should be noted that the United States still does not have a federal anti-lynching law enacted.

10. The Teeters and Zibulka (1974) inventory contains the names of the persons executed, the date of execution, the county of prosectuion, the criminal offense for which the prisoner was executed, the race and age of the prisoner, and whether the prisoner was afforded an opportunity to appeal the capital case to a higher court prior to execution. All data, other than appeal data, were supplied to Teeters and Zibulka by wardens from the records of the Departments of Corrections of the various states. The data on appeals was derived from the **Decennial Digest**. This inventory has been published as an appendix to William J. Bowers' (1974) **Executions in America**.

11. The transfer of authority from local communities to the power of the state to administrate executions characterizes a fundamental movement in the imposition of capital punishment in the United Statees. Bowers (1974) points out that with the advent of the state prison system and the concentration of penal authority with the state that states began to require that executions be performed under state authority rather than local authority. Although the first state-imposed execution occurred as early as 1853 in the District of Columbia, the movement toward state imposed executions was not readily adopted by the several states until the 1890's.

12. Studies conducted on racial discrimination in the application of the death penalty before **Furman** include Brearley (1930), Myrdal (1933), Mangum (1940), Johnson (941), Allredge (1942), Garfinkel (1949), Johnson (1957), Florida Civil Liberties Union (1964), Ohio Legislative Service Commission (1961), Wolfgang et al. (1962), Carter and Smith (1969), Judson et al. (1969), Kalven (1969), Koeninger (1969), Ehrmann (1952), McCafferty (1972), Zimring et al (1976), Bjowers (1974), **Virginia Law Review** (1972), **Jackson v. Georgia** (1972), and compare Kleck (1981).

13. The **Furman** decision basically held that all death penalty statues in the United States were unconstitutional because they permitted capital punishment to be applied in a discretionary and discriminatory manner amounting to "cruel and unusual punishment" in violation of the Eighth Amendment to the U.S. federal Constitution. The **Furman** decision did not abolish capital punishment in the United States; the court argued that the death penalty "in and of itself" does not constitute cruel and unusual punishment, but, the capricious manner in which the penalty had been applied in the cases before the court at the time of **Furman** was held unconstitutional.

14. In the **Gregg** decision, the court attempted to curb the extent to which the death penalty was applied to blacks in a discretionary and discriminatory manner by providing for guided discretion in capital sentencing. The court affirmed the death sentences of the cases under review in **Gregg** because the states from which the cases had originated, in their capital statutes, had directed attention to the circumstances of the crimes and provided for consideration of mitigating factors designed to protect against arbitrary imposition of the death penalty.

15. See Bowers and Pierce, 1980; Ekland-Olson, 1988; Radelet, 1981; Zeisel, 1981; Radelet and Pierce, 1985; Paternoster, 1983, 1984; Radelet and Vandiver, 1983; Jacoby and Paternoster, 1982; Gross and Mauro, 1984, 1989; Baldus et al., 1980a; 1980b, 1983; Baldus, 1983, 1985; Radelet and Pierce, 1985; Liegman, 1985; **McClesky v. Zant**, 1984; **McClesky v. Kemp**, 1987; Klepper et al., 1981; Thomson and Zimgraff, 1981; Vito and Keil, 1988; Hubbard, 1985; Smith, 1987; and compare Barnett, 1985; Heilburn et al., 1989.

16. McClesky claimed that race had infected the administration of capital punishment in Georgia in two distinct ways. First, "prisoners who murder whites are more likely to be sentenced to death than prisoners who murder blacks," and, secondly, "black murderers are more likely to be sentenced to death than white murderers" (McClesky, 1987). McClesky relied upon the findings of the Baldus et al. (1983) study that, in the state Georgia, killers of whites were 4.3 times more likely to be sentenced to death than killers of blacks, and black defendants were 1.1 times more likely to be sentenced to death than other defendants. McClesky held that he was discriminated against by the Georgia system of imposing the death penalty because he is a black man who killed a white.

17. In general, research has shown that public support for the death penalty is more an aspect of geneal political-social ideology than a response to crime-related concerns or experiences (Tyler and Weber, 1982; Ellsworth and Ross, 1983; Warr and Stafford, 1984). As such, public support for the death penalty become a symbolic link at the personal level with a larger body of social structures that seeks to promote the image that the death penalty is an ideological weapon against crime.

18. Finckenauer (1988) provides a detailed review of the social, political, and psychological issues surrounding public support for the death penalty.

19. For extensive review of the Court's treatment of the death penalty see the following: White (1987), Greenberg (1982), Zimring and Hawkins (1987), Gross and Mauro (1984), Amsterdam (1988).

APPENDICES

REFERENCES

Abney, Armando J. and Jane L. Moore. (1978). "A Descriptive Analysis of Social Correlates and Their Influence on Attitudes Toward the Death Penalty" (Unpublished manuscript) Southwest Texas State University.

Aikens v. California, 406 U.S. 813 (1972).

Aguirre, Adalberto, Jr. and David V. Baker. (1989). "The Execution of Mexican American Prisoners in the Southwest," **Social Justice**, 16(4):150-161.

Alderete, A. (1980). "The Use of Physical Force by Police -- A Perennial Chicano Community Dilemma." In U.S. Department of Justice, National Hispanic Conference on Law Enforcement and Criminal Justice, pp. 193-214. Washington, D.C.: Government Printing Office.

Allredge, E. P. (1942). "Why the South leads the Nation in Murder and Manslaughter." **The Quarterly Review**, 2:123.

Almaguer, T. (1971). "Toward the Study of Chicano Colonialism." **Aztlan: International Journal of Chicano Studies Research**, 2:17-22.

Alston, Jon P. (1976). "Japanese and American Attitudes Toward the Capital Punishment." **Criminology**, 14(2):271-276.

Amsterdam, A. (1988). "Race and the Death Penalty." **Criminal Justice Ethics**, 7(2):84-86.

Arkin, Steven. (1980). "Discrimination and Arbitrariness in Capital Punishment: An Analysis of Post-**Furman** Murder Cases in Dade County, Florida, 1973-1976." **Stanford Law Review** 33:75.

Baldus, David C., Charles Pulaski and George Woodsworth. (1983). "Comparative Review of Death Sentences: An Empirical Study of the Georgia Experience." **The Journal of Criminal Law Criminology**, 74(3):661-770.

_____. "Monitoring and Evaluating Contemporary Death Sentencing Systems: Lessons from Georgia." **The University of California**, Davis Law Review, 18(4):1375-1407, 1985.

Baldus, David C., Charles A. Pulaski, George Woodworth, and Frederick D. Kyle. (1980a). "Identifying Comparatively Excessive Sentences of Death: A Quantitative Approach." **Stanford Law Review** 33:1.

Barnett, Arnold. (1985). "Some Distribution Patterns for the Georgia Death Sentence." **The University of California, Davis Law Review**, 18(4):1327-1374.

Barrera, M., C. Munoz and C. Orenlas. (1972). "The Barrio as an Internal Colony." In H. Hahn (ed.), **People and Politics in Urban Society** (pp. 465-498). Beverly Hill, California: Sage Publications.

Barrera, Mario. (1979). **Race and Class in the Southwest**. Notre Dame, Indiana: University of Notre Dame Press.

Batson v. Kentucky (1986). 106 S CT. 1717, 90 L.Ed.2d 69.

Bedau, H. A. (1964). "Death Sentences in New Jersey: 1907-1960." **Rutgers Law Review** 19:1.

Bee, R. and R. Gingerich. (1977). "Colonialism, Classes and Ethnic Identity: Native Americans and the National Political Economy." **Studies in Comparative International Development**, 12:70-93.

_____. (1965). "Capital Punishment in Oregon: 1903-1964." **Oregon Law Review**, 45:1.

Bell, Derrick A. (1973). **Race, Racism, and American Law**. Boston, MA: Little Brown and Company.

Berger, R. (1989). **The Fourteenth Amendment and the Bill of Rights**. Norman, OK: University of Oklahoma Press.

Blauner, Robert. (1972). **Racial Oppression in America**. New York, NY: Harper and Row.

Bohrenstedt, George W. and Knoke, David. (1982). **Statistics for Social Data Analysis**. Chicago, IL: Peacock Publishers.

Bondavalli, B. and B. Bondavalli. (1980). "Spanish-speaking People and the North American Criminal Justice System." In R. McNeely and C. Pope (eds.), **Race, Crime and Criminal Justice**, pages 49-69. Beverly Hills, California: Sage Publications.

Bonilla, Frank and Robert Girling (eds). (1973). **Structures of Dependency**. Palo Alto, CA: Stanford University Press.

Boris, Steven B. (1979). "Stereotypes and Dispositions for Criminal Homicide," **Criminology**, 17(2):139-158.

Bowers, William J. (1974). **Executions in America**. Lexington, MA: D.C. Heath and Company.

_____. (1983). "The Pervasiveness of Arbitrariness and Discrimination Under Post-**Furman** Capital Statutes." **Crime and Delinquency**, 563:575.

Branch v. Texas (1972). 408 U.S. 238.

Brearley, H. C. (1930). "The Negro and Homicides," **Social Forces**, 9(2):247-253.

Briere, E. (1978). "Limited English Speakers and the Miranda Rights." **TESOL Quarterly**, 12:235-245.

Brooks, Roy L. (1987). "Anti-Minority Mindset in the Law School Personnel Process: Toward an Understanding of Racial Mindset." **Law and Inequality** 5(1):1-31.

Bye, Raymond T. (1919). **Capital Punishment in the United States.** Madison, WS: George Banta Publishing Company.

Campbell, Agnus. (1971). **White Attitudes Toward Black People.** Ann Arbor, MI: Institute of Social Research.

Carter, Robert M. and LaMont A. Smith. (1969). "The Death Penalty in California: A Statistical Composite Portrait." **Crime and Delinquency,** 15(1):63-76.

Carter, S. (1988). "When Victims Happen to be Black." **The Yale Law Journal,** 97:420-447.

Casanova, P. G. (1965). **Internal Colonialism and National Development.** Studies in Comparative International Development, 1(4):27-37.

Case, Charles E. and Andrew M. Greeley. (1985a). "Attitudes Toward Racial Equality." **Scientific American** (forthcoming).

Case, Charles E. and Andrew M. Greeley. (1985b). "Education, Cultural Knowledge, Social Status, and Egalitarian Attitudes Toward Blacks." (Unpublished manuscript). University of California, Riverside.

Castaneda v. Partida (1977). 430 U.S. 482.

Chadbourn, James Harmon. (1933). **Lynching and the Law.** Chapel Hill, NC: The University of North Carolina Press.

Chambliss, William. (1964). "A Sociological Analysis of the Law of Vagrancy," **Social Problems** 12 (Summer):67-77.

Chang, W. and M. Araujo. (1975). "Interpreters for the Defense: Due Process for the Non-English-Speaking Defendant." **California Law Review,** 63:801-823.

Churchill, W. (1985). "Indigenous Peoples of the United States: A Struggle Against Internal Colonialism." **Black Scholar,** 16:29-35.

Cohen, B. P. (1980). **Developing Sociological Knowledge: Theory and Method.** Englewood Cliffs, NJ: Prentice-Hall, Publishers.

Cojker v. Georgia (1977). 433 U.S. 584.

Collier, C. and J. L. Collier,. (1986). **Decision In Philadelphia: The Constitutional Convention of 1787.** New York, NY: Ballantine Books.

Combs, M. W. and J. C. Comer. (1982). "Race and Capital Punishment: A Longitudinal Analysis," **Phylon,** 4:350-359.

Comment. (1978). "Trying Non-English conversant Defendants: The Use of an Interpreter." **Oregon Law Review,** 57:549-565.

Condran, John G. (1979). "Changes in White Attitudes Toward Blacks: 1963-1977." **Public Opinion Quarterly** 43(4):463-476.

Cronheim, A. and A. Schwartz. (1976). "Non-English-Speaking Persons in the Criminal Justice System: Current State of the Law." **Cornell Law Review**, 61:289-311.

Cutler, James Elbert. (1905). **Lynch-Law: An Investigation into the History of Lynching in the United States**. New York, NY: Longsman, Green and Company.

Davidson, R. (1974). **Chicano Prisoners: The Key to San Quentin**. New York, NY: Holt, Rinehart and Winston.

Davis, James A. (1980). **General Social Survey, 1972-1980**. Chicago, IL: National Oopinion Research Center.

Davis, James Allan and Tom W. Smith. (1986). **General Social Survey, 1972-1986**. Machine readable data file. Principal Investigator, James A. Davis; Senior Study Director, Tom W. Smith. NORC ed. Chicago, IL: National Opinion Research Center, producer, 1986; Storrs, CT: Roper Public Opinion Research Center, University of Connecticut, distributor. 1 data file (17,052 logical recordes) and 1 codebook (483 pages).

Disch, Thomas M. and John Sladek. (1989). **Black Alice**. New York, NY: Carrol and Graff Publishers.

Dix, G. (1979). "Appellate Review of the Decision to Impose Death." **Georgetown Law Journal**, 68:97-161.

Duncan, Beverly and Otis Dudley Duncan. **Sex Typing and Social Roles: A Research Report**. New York, NY: Academic Press.

Duncan, H. D. (1962). **Communication and the Social Order**. New York, NY: Oxford University Press.

Ehrhardt, C. W. (1973). "The Aftermath of Furman: The Florida Experience." **The Journal of Criminal Law, Criminology, and Police Science**, 64(March):2-21.

Ehrman, H. B. (1952). "The Death Penalty and the Administration of Justice." **The Annals of the American Academy of Political and Social Science**, 284:73.

Ellsworth, P. C. and L. Ross. (1983). "Public Opinion and Capital Punishment: A Close Examination of the Views of Abolitionists and Retentionists," **Crime and Delinquency**, 29(1):116-169.

Erskine, H. B. (1970). "The Polls: Capital Punishment." **Public Oopinion Quarterly** 34:290.

Fanon, F. (1968). **The Wretched of the Earth**. New York, NY: Grove Press.

Fattah, Ezzat A. (1979). "Perception of Violence, Concerns about Crime, Fear of Victimization and Attitudes Toward the Death Penalty," **Canadian Journal of Criminology**, 21(1):22-38.

Feagin, J. (1986). "Slavery Unwilling to Die: the Background of Black Oppression in the 1980s." **Journal of Black Studies**, 17:173-200.

Feagin, J. R. and C. B. Feagin. (1978). **Discrimination American Style: Institutional Racism and Sexism**. Englewood Cliffs, NJ: Prentice-Hall, Publishers.

Feagin, Joseph R. (1984). **Racial and Ethnic Relations.** Trinton, NJ: Prentice-Hall, Publishers.

Fellman, David. (1976). **The Defendant's Rights Today.** Madison, WI: The University of Wisconsin Press.

Finckenauer, J. (1988). "Public Support for the Death Penalty: Retribution As Just Desserts or Retribution As Revenge?" **Justice Quarterly,** 5:81-100.

Fiss, O. M. (1986). "Racial Discrimination." In L. W. Levy, K. L. Karat and D. J. Mahoney (eds.), **Civil Rights and Equality,** New York, NY: MacMillan, Publishers, 17-29.

Flanagan, Timothy J. and Edmund F. McGarrell (eds). (1986). **Sourcebook of Criminal Justice Statistics - 1986.** Washington D.C.: U.S. Government Printing Office.

Florida Civil Liberties Union (1964). **Pamphlet.**

Foley, L. A. (1987). "Florida After the **Furman** Decision: The Effect of Extralegal Factors on the Processing of Capital Offense Cases," **Behavioral Sciences and the Law,** 5(4):457-465.

Furman v. Georgia (1972). 408 U.S. 238.

Gallup, George. (1978). **Public Opinion 1972-1977.** Delaware: Scholarly Resource, Inc.

The Gallup Report. (1981). April (#187).

The Gallup Report. (1985). January/February (#232/233).

Garfinkel, Harold. (1949). "Research Notes on Inter and Intra-Racial Homicides," **Social Forces,** 27:369-381.

Garza, H. (1973). "Administration of Justice: Chicanos in Monterrey County." **Aztlan: International Journal of Chicano Studies Research,** 4:137-146.

Gedicks, A. (1985). "Multinational Corporations and Internal Colonialism in the Advanced Capitalist Counties: The New Resource Wars. **Political Power and Social Theory,** 5:169-205.

Geier, James A. (1986). **The Legacy of Colonialism: A Comparative Historical Analysis of Internal Colonialism in the United States and South Africa.** (Unpublished doctoral dissertation). University of California, Riverside.

Gelles, Richard J. and Straus, Murray A. (1975). "Family Experience and Public Support for the Death Penalty." **American Journal of Orthopsychiatry** 45(4) July.

Geschwender, James A. (1978). **Racial Stratification in America.** Dubuque, Iowa: William C. Brown and Company, Publishers.

Goldberg, Arthur J. and Alan M. Dershowitz. (1970). "Declaring the Death Penalty Unconstitutional." **Harvard Law Review** 83:1773-1819 (June).

Grant, Donald L. (1975). **The Anti-Lynching Movement: 1883-1932.** San Francisco, CA: R and E Research Associates.

Greeley, Andrew M. and Paul Sheatsley. (1971). "Attitudes Toward Racial Integration." **Scientific American** 225:13-19.

Greenberg, J. (1982). "Capital Punishment as a System." **The Yale Law Journal**, 91:908-936.

Gregg v. Georgia (1976). 428 U.S. 153.

Gross, S. R. and R. Mauro. (1984). "Patterns of Death: An Analysis of Racial Disparities in Capital Sentencing and Homicide Victimization," **Stanford Law Review**, 37:27-153.

Gross, Samuel R. (1985). "Race and Death: The Judicial Evaluation of Evidence of Discrimination in Capital Sentencing." **University of California, Davis Law Review**, 18:1275-1325.

Gross, Samuel R. and Robert Mauro. (1984). "Patterns of Death: An Analysis of Racial Disparities in Capital Sentencing and Homicide Victimization." **Stanford Law Review** 37:27.

Hagan, John and Kristin Bumiller. (1983). "Making Sense of Sentencing: A Review and Critique of Sentencing Research." In Alfred Blmstein, Jacqueline Cohen, Susan E. Martin, and Michael H. Tonry (eds.). Vol. 2. National Academy Press, 1-54.

Hall, Jacquelyn Dowd. (1979). **Revolt Against Chivalry - Jessie Daniel Ames and the Women's Campaign Against Lynching**. New York, NY: Columbia University Press.

Harris, Louis. (1970). **The Harris Survey**. New York, NY: Lee Harris and Associates.

Harris, Louis. (1973). **The Harris Survey**. New York, NY: Lee Harris and Associates.

Harris, Trudier. (1984). **Exorcising Blackmen: Historical and Literary Lynching and Burning Rituals**. Bloomington, IN: Indiana University Press.

Hedderson, J. (1987). **SPSSX Made Simple**. Belmont, CA: Wadworth Publishing Company.

Hill, R. C. (1980). "Race, Class and the State: The Metropolitan Enclave System in the United States." **Insurgent Sociologist**, 10:45-59.

Hoffman, L. W. (1977). "Changes in Family Roles, Socialization and Sex Differences." **American Psychologist**, 32:644-657.

Holmes, M. and H. Daudistel. (1984). "Ethnicity and Justice in the Southwest: The Sentencing of Angle, Black, and Mexican American Defendants." **Social Science Quarterly**, 65:265-277.

Hull, C. Hadlai and Norman H. Nie. (1981). **SPSS Update 7-9 New Procedures and Facilities for Releases 7-9**. New York, NY: McGraw Hill, Inc.

Hyman, Herbert H. and Paul B. Sheatsley. (1956). "Attitudes Toward Desegregation." **Scientific American** 195:35-39.

_____. (1964). "Attitudes Toward Desegregation." **Scientific American** 211:16-23.

Jackson v. Georgia (1972). 408 U.S. 238.

Jackson, P. and L. Carroll. (1981). "Race and the War on Crime: The Sociopolitical Determinants of Municipal Police Expenditures in 90 Non-Southern U.S. Cities." **American Sociological Review** 46:290-305.

Jacobs, D. (1979). "Inequality and Police Strength: Conflict Theory and Coercive Control in Metropiolitan Areas." **American Sociological Review** 44:913-925.

Jacobson, C. K. (1984). "Internal Colonialism and Native Americans: Indian Labor in the United States from 1871 to World War II." **Social Science Quarterly,** 65:158-171.

Jacobson, Cardell K. (1985). "Resistence to Affirmative Action." **Journal of Conflict Resolution,** June 29(2):306-329.

Jacoby, Joseph E. and Raymond Paternoster. (1982). "Sentencing Disparity and Jury Packing: Further Challenges to the Death Penalaty." **The Journal of Criminal Law and Criminology,** 73(1):379-387.

Jamieson, Katherine M. and Timothy J. Flanagan, eds. (1987). **Sourcebook of Criminal Justice Statistics - 1986.** U. S. Department of Justice, Bureau of Justice Statistics. Washington D.C. : U.S. Government PRinting Office.

Jinadu, L. A. (1976). **Language and Politics: On the Cultural Basis of Colonialsim.** Cahiers d'Etudes Africaines, 16:603-614.

Johnson, Elmer. (1957). "Selective Factors in Capital Punishment. **Social Forces,** 35(2):165-169.

Johnson, Guy B. (1941). "the Negro and Crime." **The Annals of the American Academy of Political and Social Science,** 217:93-104.

Jolly, Robert W., Jr. and Edward Sagarin. (1984). "The First Eight After Furman: Who Was Executed with the Return of the Death Penalty?" **Crime and Delinquency,** October 30(4):610-623.

Judson, Charles et al. (1969). "A Study of the California Penalty Jury in First Degree Murder Cases." **Stanford Law Review,** June:1297-1497.

Jurek v. Texas (1976). 428 U.S. 262.

Kagiwada, G. (1983). "Beyond Internal Colonialism: Relflections from the Japanese American Experience." **Humboldt Journal of Social Relations,** 10:177-203.

Kinder, Donald R. and David O. Sears. (1981). "Prejudice and Politics: Symbolic Racism Versus Racial Threats to the Good Life." **Journal of Personality and Social Psychology,** 50(3):414-431.

Kleck, Gary. (1981). "Racial Discrimination in Criminal Sentencing: A Critical Evaluation of the Evidence With Additional Evidence on the Death Penalty." **American Sociological Review,** 46:783-804.

Klepper, S., D. Nagin and L. Tierney. (1981). "Discrimination in the Criminal Justice System: A Critical Appraisal of the Literature." **Research on Sentencing** 2:55.

Knoke, David and Peter J. Burke. (1978). **Log-Linear Models**. Belmont, CA: Sage Publications.

Koeninger, Rupert C. (1969). "Capital Punishment in Texas, 1924-1968." **Crime and Delinquency,** 15(1):132-141.

Kohlberg, Lawrence and Donald Elfenbein. (1976). "Moral Judgments about Capital Punishment: A Developmental-Psychological View." In Huga Adam Bedau and Chester M. Pierce (eds.) **Capital Punishment in the United States**. New York, NY: AMS Press, Inc.

LaFree, G. (1980). "The Effect of Sexual Stratification by Race on Official to Rape." **American Sociological Review** 45:842-854.

Laguerre, M. S. (1979). "Internal Dependency: The Structural Position of the Black Ghetto in American Society." **Journal of Ethnic Studies,** 6:29-44.

Lieberman, L. (1973). "The Emerging Model of the Black Family." **International Journal of Sociology of the Family,** 3:10-22.

Liebman, Ellen. (1983). "Appellate Review of Death Sentences: A Critique of Proportionality Review." **The University of California, Davis Law Review,** 18(4):1433-1480.

Litwark, Leon. (1987). "Professor Seeks Revolution of Values." **The University of California Clip Sheet,** 62(21) May.

Mandel, J. (1979). "Hispanics in the Criminal Justice System: The 'Nonexistent' Problem." **Agenda** (May/June):16-20.

Mangum, C. S. (1940). **The Legal Status of the Negro**. Chapel Hill, NC: University of North Carolina Press.

Martinez, R. (1983). "Internal Colonialism: A Reconceptualization of Race Relations in the United States." **Humboldt Journal of Social Relations,** 10:163-176.

Maxwell v. Bishop (1968). 398 F.2d 138.

McCafferty, J. A. (ed). (1972). **Capital Punishment**. New York, NY: Aldine-Atherton Company.

MeClesky v. Zant (1984). 580 F. Supp. 338, 353-79.

McClesky v. Kemp (1987). Slip Opinion #84-6811.

McConashay, John B. (1979). "Has Racism Decline in America?" **Journal of Conflic Resolution,** 25:263-279 December.

McDonald, Laughlin. (1972). "Capital Punishment in South Carolina: The End of an Era." **South Carolina Law Review,** 24(5):762-794.

McGarrel, Edmund and Timothy Flanagan. (1985). **Sourcebook of Criminal Justice Statistics - 1984**. U.S. Department of Justice, Bureau of Justice Statistics. Washington D.C.: U.S. Government Printing Office.

McGautha v. California (1968). 402 U.S. 183.

McGovern, James R. (1982). **Anatomy of a Lynching: The Killing of Claude Neal.** Baton Rouge, LA: Louisiana State University Press.

McKenna, F. R. (1981). "The Myth of Multiculturalism and the Reality of the American Indian in Contemporary America." **Journal of American Indian Education**, 21:1-9.

Memmi, A. (1965). **The Colonizer and the Colonized.** Boston, MA: Beacon Press, Inc.

Mills, C. Wright. (1959). **Sociological Imagination.** New York, NY: Oxford University Press.

Moore, Jane L. (1978). "A Descriptive Analysis of Social Correlates and Their Influence on Attitudes Toward the Death Penalty." Unpublished manuscript. Southwest Texas STate University, San Marcos.

Morales, A. (1972). **Ando Sangrando: A Study of Mexican American Police Conflict.** La Puente, CA: Perspective Publications.

Morrissey, M. (1983). "Ethnic Stratification and the Study of Chicanos." **Journal of Ethnic Studies**, 10:71-99.

Murguia, E. (1975). **Assimilation, Colonialism and the Mexican American People.** Austin, Texas: Center for Mexican American Studies, Mexican American Monograph Series #1.

Myrdal, Gunnar. (1944). **An American Dilemma: The Negro Problem and Modern Democracy.** New York, NY: Harper and Row.

National Association for the Advancement of Colored People. (1969). **Thirty Years of Lynching in the United States.** New York, NY: Arno Press.

Nie, Norman H., Hadlai C. Hull, Jean G. Jenkins, Karin Steinbrenner, and Dale H. Bent. (1975). **SPSS - Statistical for the Social Sciences**, 2nd ed. New York, NY: McGraw Hill, Inc.

Note. (1973). "Capital Punishment after Furman." **Journal of Criminal Law, Criminology and Police Science**, 64:281-289.

Ohio Legislative Service Commission. (1961). **Capital Punishment**, Staff Research Report No. 46.

Paternoster, Raymond. (1983). "Race of Victim and Location of Crime: The Decision to Seek the Death Penalty in South Carolina." **The Journal of Criminal Law and Criminology**, 74(3):754-785.

_____. (1984). "Prosecutorial Discretion in Requesting the Death Penalty: A Case of Victim-Based Racial Discrimination." **Law and Society Review**, 18(3):437-478.

Perez, W. (1985). "Constitutional Law - Translators: Mandaotry for Due Process." **Connecticut Law Review**, 2:163-170.

Petersilia, J. (1985). "Racial Disparities in the Criminal Justice System: A Summary." **Crime and Delinquency**, 31:15-34.

Phillip, Charles David. (1986). "Social Structure and Social Control: Modeling the Discriminatory Execution of Blacks in Georgia and North Carolina, 1925-1935." **Social Forces,** 65:2, December.

Pinal, J. (1973). "The Penal Population of California." In O. Romano-V. (ed.), **Voices: Readings From El Grito,** pp. 483-499. Berkeley, CA: Quinto Sol Publications, del.

Pole, J. R. (1988). "Equality: An American Dilemma." In L. Berlowitz, D. Donoghue, and L. Menand (eds.), **America in Theory.** New York, NY: Ojxford University Press, 69-83.

Proffit v. Florida (1976). 428 U.S. 242.

Radelet, Michael. (1981). "Racial Characteristics and the Imposition of the Death Penalty." **American Sociological Review,** 46:918.

_____. (1985). "Rejecting the Jury: The Imposition of the Death Penalty in Florida." **The University of California, Davis, Law Review,** 18(4):1409-1432.

Radelet, Michael and Glenn Pierce. "Race and Prosecutorial Discretion in Homicide Cases." **Law and Society Review** 19:587.

Radelet, Michael and Margaret Vandiver. "The Florida Supreme Court and Death Penalty Appeals." **The Journal of Criminal Law and Criminology** 73:913.

Rankin, Joseph H. (1979). "Changing Attitudes Toward Capital Punishment." **Social Forces** 58(1), September.

Raper, Arthur F. (1933). **The Tragedy of Lynching.** Chapel Hill, NC: The University of North Carolina Press.

Reich, Michael. (1981). **Racial Inequality.** Princeton, NJ: University Press.

Reichel, Philip L. and Lisa Munden. (1987). "Media Coverage of Executions." (unpublished manuscript), University of Northern Colorado.

Reidel, Marc. (1976). "Death Row 1975: A Study of Offenders Sentenced Under Post-**Furman** Statutes." **Temple Law Quarterly,** 49:261ff.

Reiman, Jeffrey H. (1979). **The Rich Get Richer and the Poor Get Prison.** New York, NY: John Wiley and Sons.

Roberts v. Louisiana (1976). 428 U.S. 325.

Ryder, Norman. (1965). "The Cohort as a Concept in the Study of Social Change." **American Sociological Review,** 30:843-861.

Safford, J. (1977). "No Comprendo: The Non-English-Speaking Defendant and the Criminal Process." **The Journal of Criminal Law and Criminology,** 68:15-30.

Sarat, Austin and Neil Vidmar. "Public Opinion, the Death Penalty, and the Eighth Amendment: Testing the Marshall Hypothesis," **Wisconsin Law Review,** 369.

Sears, David, Carl Hensler and Leslie Speer. (1972). "Whites' Opposition to Busing: Self-Interest vs. Symbolic Politics in Policy Attitudes and Presidential Voting," **American Political Science Review** 74:670.

Sears, David. (1971). "Political Socialization." In Ithiel de Sola Pool (ed.). **Handbook of Communication.** Chicago, IL: Rand McNally, Publishers.

Sellin, Johan Thorsten. (1980). **The Penalty of Death.** Beverly Hill, CA: Sage Publications.

Sheatsley, Paul B. (1966). "White Attitudes Toward the Negro." **Daedalus,** 95:217-238.

Simon, Rita James. (1974). **Public Opinion in America: 1930-1970.** Chicago, IL: Rand McNally.

Smith, Wade A. (1982). "White Attitudes Toward School Desegregation, 1954-1980: An Update on a Continuing Trend." **Pacific Sociological Review** 25(1):3-25 January.

Smith, T. W. (1976). "A Trend Analysis of Attitudes Toward Capital Punishment." In J. A. Davis (ed.), **Studies of Social Change Since 1948.** National Oopinion Research Center Report No. 127B.

Snead, Howard. (1986). **Blood Justice: The Lynching of Mack Charles Packer.** New York, NY: Oxford University Press.

Spinkellink v. Wainwright (1978). 578 F.2d 582 (5th Cir.).

Stanislaus Roberts v. Louisiana (1976). 428 U.S. 325.

Staples, R. (1975). "White Racism, Black Crime and American Justice: An Application of the Colonial Model to Explain Crime and Race." **Phylon,** 36:14-22.

Staples, Robert. (1976). "White Racism, Black Crime, and American Justice: An Application of the Colonial Model to Explain Crime and Race." **Phylon,** 7(1):14-22.

Stinchcombe, Arthur, Rebecca Adams, Carol Heimer, Kim Scheppele, Tom Smith and Garth D. Taylor. (1980). **Crime and Punishment: Changing Attitudes in America.** San Francisco, CA: Josse-Bass, Publications.

Swigert, Victoria Lynn and Ronald A. Farrell. (1976). **Murder, Inequality and the Law: Differential Treatment in the Legal Process.** Lexington, MA: D.C. Heath.

_____. (1977). "Normal Homicides and the Law," **American Sociological Review,** February:16-32.

Takaki, R. (1979). **Iron Cages: Race and Culture in 19th Century America.** Seattle, WA: University of Washington Press.

Taylor, Garth D.j, Paul B. Sheatsley and Andrew M. Greeley. (1978). "Attitudes Toward Racial Integration." **Scientific American** 238:42-49 June.

Taylor, Garth D., Kim Sheppele and Arthur Stinchcombe. (1979). "Salience of Crime and Support for Harsher Criminal Sanctions," **Social Problems** 26:413.

Teetets, N. K. and C. J. Zibulka. (1974). "Executions Under State Authority." In William J. Bowers **Executions in America**. Lexington, MA: D.C. Heath and Company.

The Riverside Press-Enterprise. (1987). "Death Penalty Upheld Despite Racial Disparities," (Thursday), April 23.

The Riverside Press-Enterprise. (1987). "High Court Justice Rips Constitution and Its Authors," (Thursday), May 7.

Thomas, Charles. (1977). "Eighth Amendment Challenges to the Death Penalty; The Relevance of Informed Public Opinion," **Vanderbilt Law Review** 30:1005.

Thomas, Charles and Robin Cage. (1976). "Correlates of Public Attitudes Toward Legal Sanctions," **International Journal of Criminology and Penology** 4:239.

Thomas, Charles and Robert Howard. (1977). "Public Attitudes Toward Capital Punishment: A Comparative Analysis," **Journal of Behavioral Economics** 6:189.

Thomas, Charles and Samuel Foster. (1975). "A Sociological Perspective on Public Support for Capital Punishment." **American Journal of Orthopsychiatry** 45(4):641-657 July.

Thomson, Randall and Mathew T. Zimgraff. (1981). "Detecting Sentencing Disparity: Some Problems and Evidence." **American Journal of Sociology** 86:869.

Turner, Jonathan H., Royce Singleton, Jr. and David Musick. (1984). **Oppression: A Socio-History of Black-White Relations in America**. Chicago, IL: Nelson-Hall, Publishers.

Tyler, Tom R. and Renee Weber. (1982). "Support for the Death Penalty: Instrumental Response to Crime, or Symbolic Attitude?" **Law and Society Review**, 17(1):21-45.

United States Commission on Civil Rights. (1970). **Mexican Americans and the Administration of Justice in the Southwest**. Washington, D.C.: U.S. Government Printing Office.

United States Department of Justice. (1980). **National Hispanic Conference on Law Enforcement and Ccriminal Justice**. Washington, D.C.: U.S. Government Printing Office.

Vidmar, Neil. (1974). "Retributive and Utilitarian Motives and Other Correlates of Canadian Attitudes Toward the Death Penalty," **The Canadian Psychologist** 15:337.

Vidmar, Neil and Dale Miller. (1980). "Sociopsychological Processes Underlying Attitudes Toward Legal Punishment," **Law and Society Review** 14:564.

Virginia Law Review. (1972). "Capital Punishment in Virginia." **Virginia Law Review**, 58:97.

Warr, M. and M. Stafford. (1984). "Public Goals of Punishment and Support for the Death Penalty," **Journal of Research in Crime and Delinquency**, 21(2):95-111.

Welch, S., J. Gruhl and C. Spohn. (1984). "Dismissal, Conviction, and Incarceration of Hispanic Defendants: A Comparison with Anglos and Blacks." **Social Science Quarterly**, 65:257-264.

Wells-Barnett, Ida B. (1969). **On Lynchings**. New York, NY: Arno Press.

White, C. E. (1981). "The Peripheralization of Blacks in Capitalist America: The Crisis of Black Youth Unemployment and the Perpetuation of Racism." Catalyst, 3:115-128.

White, W. (1987). "Patterns in Capital Punishment." California Law Review, 75:2165-2185.

White, W. S. (1987). The Death Penalty in the Eighties: An Examination of the Modern System of Capital Punishment. Ann Arbor, MI: University of Michigan Press.

White, Walter. (1929). Rope and Faggot. New York, NY: Arno Press.

Williams, Dennis A., Jerry Buckley and Mary Lord. (1979). "A New Radical Poll." Newsweek, February 26:48, 53.

Williams, Frank P., Dennis Longmire, Salida Mukora, David Gulick. (1985). "The Public and the Death Penalty: Opinion as an Artifact of Question Type." Unpublished manuscript. Indiana University of Pennsylvania.

Wolf, Edwin. (1964). "Abstract of Analysis of Jury Sentencing in Capital Cases: New Jersey 1937-1961." Rutgers Law Review Fall:56-64.

Wolfgang, Marvin and B. Cohen. (1970). Crime and Race Conceptions and Misconceptions. New York, NY: Institute of Human Relations Press.

Wolfgang, Marvin and Marc Reidel. (1973). "Race, Judicial Discretion, and the Death Penalty." The Annals of the American Academy of Political and Social Science 45:658.

Wolfgang, Marvin E., Arlene Kelley, Hans C. Nolde. (1962). "Comparison of the Executed and the Commuted Among Admissions to Death Row." The Journal of Criminal Law, Criminology, and Police Science 53(3):301-311.

Woodson v. North Carolina (1976). 428 U.S. 280.

Yinger, J. M. (1985). "Ethnicity." Annual Review of Sociology 11:151-1880.

Zangrando, Robert L. (1980). The NAACP Crusade Against Lynching, 1909-1950. Philadelphia, PA: Temple University Press.

Zatz, M. (1981). "Differential Treatment Within the Criminal Justice System by Race/Ethnicity." Paper presented at the Annual Meeting of the American Sociological Association (August) Toronto, Canada.

Ziesel, Hans. (1981). "Race Bias in the Administration of the Death Penalty: The Florida Experience." Harvard Law Review 95:456.

Zimring, Franklin, Sheila O'Malley, and Joel Eigen. "The Going Price of Criminal Homicide in Philadelphia." University of Chicago Law Review, 43:277ff.

Zimring, F. E. and G. Hawkins. (1987). Capital Punishment and the American Agenda. New York, NY: Cambridge University Press.

ABOUT THE AUTHORS

Adalberto Aguirre, Jr., Ph.D., is an Associate Professor of Sociology at the University of California, Riverside. His research interests cover the areas of sociolinguistics, sociology of education, and race and ethnic relations. His work has appeared in such journals as **Social Problems, Social Science Journal, Social Science Quarterly, Iinternational Journal of the Sociology of Language**, and **La Revue Rnemaine de Linguistique**. He is also the author of **An Experimental Sociolinguistic Investigation of Chicano Bilingualism, Intelligence Testing, Education and Chicanos**, and **Language in the Chicano Speech Community**.

David V. Baker, Ph.D., is Associate Professor and Chair of the Department of Sociology and Anthropology at Riverside Community College in Riverside, California. His research and teaching interests are in social inequality with emphasis on race and ethnic relations, large scale organizations and institutions, and criminology. Professor Baker has contributed works to several journals including the **Journal of Ethnic Studies, The Justice Professional**, the **Social Science Journal**, and the **Criminal Justice Abstracts**. With Professor Aguirre, he is presently working on a new book concerning the relationship between race and crime in the United States.

An Introduction To Gangs

George W. Knox
Foreword by Malcolm W. Klein

Concerning this Book...

Some have said it could not be done: to review and
tie together in a single textbook the extensive historical
literature and research dealing with gangs. This book
does just that. Consisting of 22 chapters on all major areas
of interest, research, programs, and policy dealing with
gangs. It also includes new national research findings
reported here for the first time.

The focus is practical, the view is social scientific, it is com-
prehensive, interdisciplinary and state-of-the-art regarding
gangs. "...the single most thorough analysis of gangs yet
produced and available today..." Professor Thomas
McCurrie, member, Academy of Criminal Justice Sciences.

Concerning the Author...

George W. Knox teaches in the Department of Corrections
and Criminal Justice, Chicago State University (Ph.D.,
University of Chicago, 1978; M.A., University of Texas
at Arlington, 1975; B.A.S., University of Minnesota, 1974).
He is certified beyond the Ph.D. in "Law and Social Control"
by the American Sociological Association and is a Certified
Consultant by the American Correctional Association.

He is a member of a variety of national groups (American
Society of Criminology, American Correctional Association,
National Criminal Justice Association, American Probation
and Parole Association, Academy of Criminal Justice
Sciences, National Juvenile Detention Association,
Midwestern Criminal Justice Association, etc).

His other publications include research on youthful and
adult offenders, and rehabilitation programs. His current
research program is the national picture regarding gangs.

VANDE VERE PUBLISHING LTD.

ISBN 0-9628916-1-4